*Nu*

MW01001629

As I read Larry Jackson's new book, I recognized immediately how the Church falls short in understanding the full meaning of the suffering of Christ. This book vividly shows that His suffering was not an end but a means to an end. It unfolds the drama of a great divine plan hidden within the garden and Cross experience that we as the Body of Christ must learn and implement throughout our lives. Jesus died for us, but we must live for Him. There is pure gold within the pages of this book, and I will now be "numbered with the transgressors."

BOBBYE BYERLY
DIRECTOR OF PRAYER, WORLD PRAYER CENTER
COLORADO SPRINGS, COLORADO

Numbered with the Transgressors will help raise the Body of Christ to a greater level of spiritual maturity in the midst of the modern prayer movement. Many will discover a desire for more of God, while others learn to walk more humbly before Him and each other.

REV. PAT CHEN
FOUNDER AND PRESIDENT, FIRST LOVE MINISTRIES INTERNATIONAL

I have witnessed firsthand the working of these truths. If you want to stay the same, put this book down now. Its contents are guaranteed to change your life.

MICHAEL FLETCHER
DIRECTOR, PRAYER NETWORK CENTER
SENIOR PASTOR, MANNA CHURCH
FAYETTEVILLE, NORTH CAROLINA

PRAISE FOR

NUMBERED WITH THE TRANSGRESSORS

We want to see revival and renewal come to our cities and our nation. But are we willing to pay the price to see our vision become a reality? Do we even know what the price is? Larry Jackson outlines for us a key factor in seeing our family, friends, cities and nation come to a true knowledge of Christ: numbering ourselves with the transgressors. I highly encourage you to read this book.

JOHN P. KELLY

FOUNDER AND OVERSEEING APOSTLE,
ANTIOCH CHURCHES AND MINISTRIES
SOUTHLAKE, TEXAS

Numbered with the Transgressors is a great work that will reach to the depths of your spirit. You will experience conviction and compassion and learn to pray with new authority. There is a birthing energy in this book that will unlock the doors to captives who have been shut away for decades.

CHUCK D. PIERCE

DIRECTOR, WORLD PRAYER CENTER
COLORADO SPRINGS, COLORADO

Read this book and put fire and compassion back into your prayers—and get results! This is an excellent guide to intercession written by a man who practices what he preaches.

SERGIO SCATAGLINI

PASTOR, PUERTA DEL CIELO
LA PLATA, ARGENTINA

NUMBERED WITH THE TRANSGRESSORS

TO TRULY INTERCEDE EFFECTIVELY
WE MUST CHOOSE TO BE...

NUMBERED WITH THE TRANSGRESSORS

CHANGING THE WAY WE SEE THE LOST
—AND OURSELVES

LARRY JACKSON

Renew

A Division of Gospel Light
Ventura, California, U.S.A.

Published by Renew Books
A Division of Gospel Light
Ventura, California, U.S.A.
Printed in U.S.A.

Renew Books is a ministry of Gospel Light, an evangelical Christian publisher dedicated to serving the local church. We believe God's vision for Gospel Light is to provide church leaders with biblical, user-friendly materials that will help them evangelize, disciple and minister to children, youth and families.

It is our prayer that this Renew book will help you discover biblical truth for your own life and help you meet the needs of others. May God richly bless you.

For a free catalog of resources from Renew Books and Gospel Light please call your Christian supplier, or contact us at 1-800-4-GOSPEL or at www.gospellight.com.

Cover Design by Kevin Keller
Interior Design by Robert Williams
Edited by Ron Durham and Virginia Woodard

Library of Congress Cataloging-in-Publication Data
Jackson, Larry, 1958–
    Numbered with the transgressors / Larry Jackson.
        p.   cm.
    ISBN 0-8307-2196-7 (trade paper)
    1. Intercessory prayer—Christianity.   2. Jesus Christ—Passion
    I. Title.
    BV215.J3 1999   98-42320
    248.3'2—dc21   CIP

1 2 3 4 5 6 7 8 9 10 11 12 13 14 15 / 04 03 02 01 00 99 98

Rights for publishing this book in other languages are contracted by Gospel Literature International (GLINT). GLINT also provides technical help for the adaptation, translation and publishing of Bible study resources and books in scores of languages worldwide. For further information, write to GLINT at P.O. Box 4060, Ontario, CA 91761-1003, U.S.A. You may also send e-mail to Glintint@aol.com, or visit their web site at www.glint.org.

CONTENTS

FOREWORD

The first time I saw how serious Larry Jackson was about God was after a long phone conversation, when I found out that he had been standing the whole time in the freezing rain at a pay phone—without an umbrella. He had never let on to me that he was getting drenched, because he was so hungry to get a good soaking from the Spirit of God.

Larry Jackson is someone who gives me hope for a new awakening in the inner cities of America. He is a product of Richmond, Virginia, from the tough Church Hill neighborhood, and growing up he did all the things you do when you are sold out to the devil. But God is alive! Jesus is real! Jesus came to Larry Jackson, and now he is sold out to God—a man of God for this generation.

Larry has a hunger for God's presence like few men I know. When he writes about prayer, he isn't just saying things that sound good. He is living the life. I have seen him in prayer totally broken and crying before a crowd because he was so moved by the sins and infirmities of the people for whom he was praying.

Over the years, Larry has been there with us on three-day prayer shut-ins, all-night prayer and 5:00 A.M. prayer on weekday mornings. He has fasted. He has gone to the prisons. He has started ministries. He has consecrated his marriage to the Lord according to the model of Christ and the Church. When I encouraged him to start planting churches, he left everything and went to another state every Sunday, commuting several hours a week until he could move his family. As that church has been established, he has been raising up disciples to start other churches in the area, then moving to plant more churches somewhere else.

Jesus had the three, the Twelve, the Seventy and the multitudes. It is like that with me, too, and Larry is right in there with my closest disciples—wanting all he can get of God from me. He models the servant lifestyle, and he can take correction like a man—even wanting more. When I became a Promise Keepers stadium speaker, it wasn't long before they were calling him to be a stadium speaker, too. We are in a holy competition to go up another level in God.

When a man spends time in the Lord's presence, you can see it in his eyes. Larry Jackson is one of those men. His eyes burn with the fire of a holy dedication that lets the generation know he is seeing in another world, and doing the mission of another world. And that mission is from heaven.

Bishop Wellington Boone
Pastor, First International Church of Atlanta
Duluth, Georgia

INTRODUCTION

In the summer of 1990, as I was beginning a personal retreat at a hotel on the beach at Virginia Beach, Virginia, a desire arose within my heart to study the suffering of Jesus. Little did I know that the Holy Spirit would use my experience to revolutionize my own prayer life and enable me to communicate the insights I am about to share with you in this book.

I had gone on the retreat with a limited agenda—sleep and mental rest. Because I can never leave behind my relationship with God and my desire to know more of Him, I had brought along my Bible, of course, and some other books—my "Kingdom tools."

Easter was now long passed, and I had no idea why God seemed to be impressing on me to become further acquainted with our Lord's experience of identifying with sinful humanity and becoming "numbered with the transgressors" (Isa. 53:12) as He gave His life for us on the cross. My first thought concerning this desire was that the Holy Spirit wanted to give me additional insight into the suffering of Jesus for a sermon the week following my time away. How wrong I was!

Once I started to study the Scriptures concerning Jesus' suffering, it became even more apparent that the Spirit was leading me, for I began to see the self-giving ministry of Jesus on the cross in a fresh and new way. With this new

insight came an excitement; but I still did not fully understand that my life would never be the same. The more I read,
it seemed my understanding became more and more fruitful.

Then, all of a sudden, it happened. For the first time in
my life I could see how Jesus' sufferings related to intercessory prayer.

I had been exposed to the principles and practice of
intercessory prayer for years, under the ministry and leadership of Bishop Wellington Boone at Manna Christian
Fellowship in Richmond, Virginia. Every day members of
our church family spent from 5:00 A.M. to 7:00 A.M. in
prayer. In these prayer times, several women such as
Mother Tindall, who led the intercessory prayer team,
would travail in prayer for hours.

Now, at my retreat, this background helped me relate
intercessory prayer to the suffering of Christ as predicted
in Isaiah 53. It was as though scales were removed from my
eyes as I saw that the two principles are one and the same.
Yet, although I had a level of excitement, a sense of cau-
tion also came upon me. With new concepts comes a level
of resistance and sometimes even rejection before they are
adopted. In no way did I want to add anything unscriptur-
al to the marvelous way intercessory prayer has come to
link all believers worldwide.

"REST" INSTEAD OF A RETREAT

So it was with cautious excitement that I pursued this time
of study. The retreat time, as I once envisioned it, was no
more. The "rest of God" was beginning to take over. There
was no doubt in my heart or mind that the Holy Spirit was
my Instructor during this special time. As the days went by,
I would take some breaks from my studies, either by taking a walk or going out to eat. Yet, inwardly, I yearned to
return to my study because my time of departure was
drawing near.

The main Scripture reference the Spirit used like a sharp knife to drive His point deep within my heart was that passage in Isaiah 53. There, Isaiah looks down through the stream of time and foresees how the coming Messiah would condescend to count Himself as one of us, and to vicariously suffer for our sins. Again, it was the latter part of verse 12 that was drilled into my mind:

> He poured out his life unto death, and was numbered with the transgressors. For he bore the sin of many, and made intercession for the transgressors.

Suddenly this verse triggered a memory of an incident that had taken place four years earlier. As I will relate in chapter 1, it was an event that showed me how to connect intercessory prayer with Christ's experience on the cross. Now, on my retreat, I was shocked at how I thought the incident was forgotten, and how the Spirit was bringing it to my remembrance again.

I became aware that although we pray for sinners, saying we love them but hate their sin, we do not actually identify with them, as Christ identified with us. We pray for transgressors in our world, in our own land and in our cities—even people in our churches and our families. But we seem to carefully avoid them—certainly we would never want to be seen with them in public! In other words, it appears that in many cases we not only hate the sin but the sinner!

My experience on that retreat at Virginia Beach made me question whether those attitudes are Christlike. After all, as Christians we are to be like Him; and He was *numbered with the transgressors*—because He loved them.

I believe that one of the greatest ways to demonstrate love for transgressors today is through the vehicle of prayer. If we want to show people outside of the church that we love them, then regular prayers must be prayed for them. Then, when Father God gives us an opportunity to speak into the lives of these that are trapped in sin, those for whom we have prayed, they will hear the voice of love and not hate, thereby causing our instruction and words of correction not to fall on deaf ears.

The ride home from my retreat was full of excitement about what God had allowed me to see. The passion that would bring others into the understanding of this revelation was causing me almost to burst. It is my prayer that what I describe in the following pages—which I now call the "Numbered with the Transgressors" principle—will also ignite a fire in your own heart, and set aflame the prayers you pray for others.

HOW GOD USED MY MISTAKE TO PLANT A PRINCIPLE

Before answering the call of God to full-time ministry, I worked for the National Education Corporation (NEC) as an electronics instructor. I was always vocal about my love for Jesus and for Kingdom standards. Because of this, several NEC staff members and students had come to know the Lord as their Savior. Of course, there were also those who, without saying anything in a direct way, wished I would keep my Kingdom stands to myself. Never did I force anything down the throats of the people around me, but neither would I allow them to force their lifestyles and/or choices down mine.

Now at this time the Church was just coming through the rough place created by the conviction of Jim Bakker for his involvement in the multimillion-dollar Heritage USA and Inspirational Network scam. Suddenly, the people who love to use other people's problems to justify their sins and resistance to Christ had a new weapon. They saw a well-known television evangelist, who spoke about a Jesus who could save people out of the grips of sin, fall into sin himself.

Then, only months after the Bakker fall, Jimmy Swaggart, who looked into the camera and warned the

United States about its moral decline, was found in a sexual sin. Jimmy Swaggart's fall also sent shock waves through the Christian community. Everyone wanted to know what was causing these Christian preachers, who were married and considered quite successful, to fall in this area.

GETTING THEM "TOLD"

I was eating lunch in the teachers' lounge at work several days following the headline news about Jimmy Swaggart's fall. Several of my coworkers came into the lunchroom and began questioning me about the fall of this nationally and internationally known television evangelist. The answer I gave that day was one being used around the world by the Church of Jesus Christ: "God is still God, and He is not surprised by any of this that is taking place. The Church of Jesus Christ will survive all of this. You should get your eyes off of Jimmy Swaggart and put them on your own spiritual condition."

These statements caused my fellow workers to take a step back, and I walked out of the room feeling as though I had "really told them."

Now fast-forward to the time of my Virginia Beach retreat, when I remembered this event. This was the first time I had remembered the incident—maybe because I thought my actions were correct, or possibly because, down deep, I suspected they were not correct. At any rate, the Holy Spirit was beginning to use things in my life, past and present, to further drill home this "Numbered with the Transgressors" principle. I thought of Jesus' promise in John:

> "But the Counselor, the Holy Spirit, whom the Father will send in my name, will teach you all things and will remind you of everything I have said to you" (John 14:26).

Although the remembrance of that event at my workplace shocked me, it was now clear how it fit perfectly with the principle God showed me while I was studying Isaiah 53. Here Jesus had numbered Himself with the transgressors, while I had found satisfaction in telling off my coworkers! Suddenly shame filled my heart and words of repentance filled my mouth when I realized how unlike Christ I had been.

Now the Spirit used the memory of this incident to cause even a greater determination to study everything the Bible had to say about intercessory prayer patterned after the way Jesus had identified with us by numbering Himself as a sinner. I bought books about intercession to expand my knowledge, but none of them related prayer to the sufferings of Jesus. It seemed to me that I was on my own; but I was to realize the Holy Spirit would continue to give me understanding and opportunity to learn and to teach what He had taught me.

A RADIO BREAKTHROUGH

At this time, my family and I were planting a new church in Fayetteville, North Carolina. Armed with this fresh Numbered with the Transgressors revelation, I taught it on my new daily radio program.

This program, which enabled me to become better known in the city, was designed to have Christians all over the city stop for 15 minutes and pray with me for revival, after a short time of instruction about prayer and revival. Until that time, we had received very few responses from the listening audience. Now and then someone would tell me they had listened and enjoyed the program, but that was it. On several occasions I asked the listening audience to write responses about the program. I offered tapes and other kinds of ministry materials as well, again having very limited success.

The program had aired on the station for several months before I began to teach out of this new insight on prayer and the sufferings of Christ. At the end of the first week I had spent presenting the principle, my mailbox held several requests for the tape. This was an encouragement to my staff and me. The responses helped me further realize that this message was not just for me, but that God's breath was on this message and the Church needed to hear it.

The responsibilities of establishing a new home and a new ministry began to mount. We had to find a new house in Fayetteville, sell our home in Richmond, find a place other than a hotel to conduct services, and many other things. With so many new responsibilities, time seemed to get away from me—and so did the message that caused the radio listening audience to respond when nothing else did. Thank God for His faithfulness and willingness to put up with us when we get so busy doing work for Him that we stop working with Him—for I was to have another opportunity.

IDENTIFYING WITH SINNERS

One Sunday, while praying for the evening church service, a very strange thing happened to me. Although what I am about to share with you really happened to me, I am in no way trying to set a precedent. Neither am I suggesting that a person must go through what I went through to walk in this principle, because I had not walked in it myself before the Holy Spirit led me into it. I share it here because many intercessors from different walks of life have told me they were relieved to hear that someone understood what they had experienced, but hadn't known what to do with it.

By this time, I was no longer broadcasting on the radio but was focusing all of my time on the new church. One Sunday evening, during a time of prayer for our church service and for God's favor on the church, without warning I began to feel like someone who lived the life of a homosexual man. This caused me to immediately stop praying to evaluate what was happening to me. Besides the fact that I had never struggled with my sexuality, I was very happily married. Nevertheless, these feelings were very real and caused me some concern, at first.

Then I began to reason that perhaps someone experiencing this problem was present in the service, and that God was showing me through what I was feeling that this person needed help in being set free from the bondage of homosexuality.

How could I come to this conclusion so quickly? Many times while ministering the Word of God, I would feel pain in my body and know someone in the audience was experiencing it. How did I know, you ask? I don't know. I just knew! The first time this happened and the Holy Spirit instructed me to tell the audience, the fear of looking foolish almost stopped me from expressing it. Since then there have been times when no one in the audience responded, but the percentage of people who do respond is fairly high. Once they respond, I pray for them, and many times they experience relief from that pain. On many occasions I have also told the audience when the pain started, how long they had been experiencing it, and on what side or which arm or leg the pain was located. This is not something I can work up, or even for the most part know when it will happen.

At any rate, I concluded that these feelings of homosexuality were like those that came to me on behalf of people in pain. Someone must have been in the service that night who needed deliverance from homosexuality. Then, to my surprise, I realized that not even one visitor was present at the service. So I dismissed what had happened to me as something unexplainable.

Days later, however, in another location with a new prayer focus, the same feelings came over me again. Our next service was days away. I was as confused this time as I had been the first time. On this occasion, however, I prayed to the Lord about the experience. I asked Him if He would help me understand what was happening.

Two Scripture references seemed to come into my mind: the fifty-third chapter of Isaiah and the eighth chapter of Romans—two of the chapters I had studied during the retreat in Virginia Beach. Suddenly a flood of understanding seemed to be released out of a dam and to overflow my soul. Although I thought the Holy Spirit was finished teaching me this principle, I found I had turned away to focus on what I thought was important. It now became crystal clear that He was using this prayer experience to further show me what He wanted me to understand months earlier: how to be numbered with the transgressors, and to identify with them and their lifestyle in intercessory prayer.

To say the least, God had my attention now. I wanted to understand what I had neglected to follow up, and what seems to be ignored by a large portion of the Body of Christ.

WHY HOMOSEXUALITY?

Maybe you are asking why God chose to use the specific transgression of homosexuality to drive home the point to my soul. For one thing, it got my full attention! The Lord had a much greater reason and plan, however, which unfolded months after this experience. Gradually these words from the Holy Spirit began to grip my heart: *I allowed you to experience in seed form what homosexual people experience so that you would learn to pray for them from their vantage point; so that you would cry out in prayer with sincerity and understanding for their deliverance.*

What I did not realize at the time has now become crystal clear. I must tell the entire Body of Christ that they are called to be numbered with transgressors for the sake of more adequately interceding for them.

Let's look again at that foundational passage of Scripture given to me at my retreat:

> Therefore I will give him a portion among the great, and he will divide the spoils with the strong, because he poured out his life unto death, and was numbered with the transgressors. For he bore the sin of many, and made intercession for the transgressors (Isa. 53:12).

Christ did not come to earth clothed in glory. He came wearing the clothes of humanity in order to identify with all that humans had experienced or ever will experience.

I believe that "the strong" in this passage refers to the Church—those who receive their strength from the Lord who saves them. In His victory over sin, Christ divides the spoils with us, giving us the strength to do what He did. Because He was numbered with the transgressors, He calls us to do the same.

In becoming a man, then dying on the cross for the sins of others, Jesus became a part of every evil work ever done on the face of the earth. Not that Christ ever sinned, but He took on the sins of all who had. In the Incarnation, Christ became guilty by association. He did not come to earth as an angel or even God, clothed in glory. He came wearing the clothes of humanity in order to totally identify with all that humans had experienced or ever will experience.

During His earthly ministry, which this book will investigate in later chapters, the religious leaders could not understand why Christ would fellowship with, eat with and go into the homes of known sinners. He even allowed a very loose woman to touch Him, which truly alarmed those religious leaders watching. These leaders began to ask the disciples of Christ if He knew who this woman was. "'If this man were a prophet,' said Simon the Pharisee, 'he would know who is touching him and what kind of woman she is—that she is a sinner'" (Luke 7:39).

Never would Simon or the other Pharisees allow this woman even to come close to them with her sin because of their position in the religious community. These religious leaders lived their lives above the people, even though they were people. Jesus, on the other hand, even though He was God's Son, not only let this sinful woman touch Him, but He also defended her actions toward Him. He was clothed in flesh, and He was willing to identify with others in the flesh.

INTENSITY IN PRAYER

Once I started praying with this new insight, the intensity of my prayer time increased so much and so fast that it shocked me. I was not only praying for the person or the situation, but I could also sense what the person was feeling. I could feel the pressure of his or her circumstance. It seemed as though that circumstance was mine; and this resulted in more intensity as I interceded.

Sometimes a person will ask for prayer, and those who are asked to pray for that person or situation will forget to pray. We will never forget to pray when we truly understand the pain of others, however, because we can feel the discomfort associated with the need. Being able to feel the need while praying causes the circumstance prayed for to become a part of the pray-er's life, thereby resulting in a deeper, more fervent prayer,

In no way am I suggesting that we should repent for other people, or even think we are that person. We are not to attempt to bear the sin burden of another person, because someone named Jesus, who is the Christ, has completed that job. We are to approach the problem with a new compassion, though, and desire to see the transgressor delivered, saved, healed and increased, as though we wanted these things personally.

By now, my passion and excitement to teach the Church this principle was fueled by this new level of prayer. I fervently hoped that it would work in their lives as it had worked in mine.

PROOF OF THE PRINCIPLE

For a long time I thought the Numbered with the Transgressors principle was a message to bring the Church back to its lost compassion for lost people. What I knew but had not connected to this principle is the fact that prayer works. Testimonies started to come in about people's loved ones' attitudes and lives changing, many of them giving their lives to Christ. All at once the results seemed to be instant. A person or a group of people would pray following my instructions, and testimonies would follow immediately.

As I mentioned, my first opportunity to share the principle was on my local radio program. Without having the experiences and insights that came later, I did not really know what to tell my audience about how to apply this principle to everyday situations. I did, however, understand the need. I knew what the Church needed to do in prayer for fallen leaders and others who are hurting—those on whom we had turned our backs.

The positive response of the listening audience greatly surprised me. Since then, not only has my own experience grown, but many testimonies from others have also been shared. Throughout this book you will read of how, through prayer and the Numbered with the Transgressors principle, lives have changed and people have been saved.

Now let me tell you about what happened the first time I shared this principle before a live audience.

PRACTICAL EFFECTS OF JOINING IN CHRIST'S SUFFERING

The first time I had the opportunity to share what I was learning about intercessory prayer came in front of a live audience at Manna Christian Fellowship in Richmond, Virginia, where Bishop Wellington Boone served as pastor. Although this was also my home church, there was additional pressure because I had never shared this principle while looking into the faces of my listeners.

As the Numbered with the Transgressors principle unfolded and became clearer, people in the congregation began to cry uncontrollably. This was not ordinary crying; it had a different sound. These people were crying just as I had cried while praying for those caught in the grip of homosexuality.

Then it happened! The church was filled with the presence of the Holy Spirit and I knew it was time for me to stop speaking, although I was not finished. By this time, His glorious presence had overtaken me also, and through my tears I instructed the congregation to pray for a family member who had not come into a relationship with Jesus Christ. I asked them to be sure they prayed from the position from which Christ offered Himself, numbering themselves with that lost person.

Once the entire congregation started praying this way, their hearts seemed to break, and the sounds of people crying aloud filled the room. At the end of the service, we all marveled at how God's Spirit had taken over the prayer time. This was a church that was committed to prayer, praying at the church daily at 5:00 A.M. and offering prayer for shut-ins every month. Yet several people indicated that they had never prayed that way before. It was not hard for me to believe that this kind of prayer was new for them, because the same thing was happening to me every time I prayed with this attitude of being "numbered." Some of the people indicated they better understood what intercession was, and how to intercede.

WHAT GOOD DOES IT DO?

Now, although you may find all this intriguing, you may also be asking one major question: What good will it do for me to identify with a loved one in sin or in situations of life that are separate from my life? Allow me to share another testimony, which connects this principle to my life even further.

One day while I was praying, I began to feel as though God did not exist. As you can imagine, this caught my attention as quickly as the time I identified with the problem of homosexuality. At the same time, my brother was going through very rough times in his life. Family members suspected he was using drugs regularly. Distance prevented me from being able to consistently spend time with him.

On this particular day, the Holy Spirit placed this thought in my mind: *Your brother's true problem is not drugs; he does not believe in God. Now you know how he feels, so pray from his vantage point.*

Two weeks later, my brother called me. He explained to me how he thought his life was trapped because of his bondage to drugs. Could I help him? Glory to God, I had already been allowed to help him by being numbered with the transgressors! Today, my brother is married, a father, free from drugs and born again.

Most of us have people in our lives who need help, and it often seems as though no one or nothing has been able to help them. I believe that God has revealed the Numbered with the Transgressors principle so we can help these helpless people come into freedom and a relationship with Him.

HEIGHTENED PRAYER LIFE

Another important fact about being numbered with transgressors, once people embrace it, is that their prayer lives seem to increase instantly. If this principle served as a means of increasing prayer in the Church, I would be more than satisfied.

Many Christians today struggle with maintaining a consistent prayer life. Although there are many reasons for this deficiency, I believe two of the main factors in this absence of the desire to pray are the lack of enjoyment and the lack of answers to prayer.

Once people start to have their prayers answered, then they will pray more. Answered prayers also cause people to enjoy the time they spend in prayer because they know it is not in vain. In the meetings where I have had an opportunity to teach this principle, I share with those praying that to see lasting change in the person(s) or situation(s) prayed for, they must *continue* to pray steadfastly.

Family members who are resisting God can be changed when someone within that family who knows God cares enough to intercede for them at this level. Those yearning to see change in their city can use this principle, and changes will happen. Those who want more intense and effective prayer lives will find that this principle will bring positive results in days and weeks as opposed to years.

Once we become a part of what we pray for, a new attitude develops. Those who have learned to apply this principle report that they have never before prayed with such intensity.

The Bible tells us in the book of James the importance and power of such prayer:

> Confess your faults one to another, and pray one for another, that ye may be healed. The effectual fervent prayer of a righteous man availeth much (5:16, *KJV*).

Many people, however, have had a difficult time realizing the necessity of continuing in *fervent* prayer. Look at how *The Amplified Bible* emphasizes this principle:

> Confess to one another therefore your faults (your slips, your false steps, your offenses, your sins) and pray [also] for one another, that you may be healed and restored [to a spiritual tone of mind and heart]. The earnest (heartfelt, continued) prayer of a righteous man makes tremendous power available [dynamic in its working].

Experienced intercessors have found a new intensity once they number themselves with another individual in prayer. This could explain in seed form why Jesus prayed for three hours in the garden, sweating great drops of blood, and the angels had to come and minister to Him. As long as you keep your heart and mind open to the Holy

Spirit, He will help you understand and move into this position of intensive prayer.

WHAT DOES IT LOOK LIKE?

In the garden of Gethsemane, Jesus experienced sorrow and pain because He had done nothing wrong. He was there for us so that we would be set free from *our* guilt, sorrow and pain. It was this vicarious suffering of Jesus that Isaiah 53 had envisioned so long before Christ's experience in the garden. The prophets, scribes and religious leaders studied this book with anticipation of Christ's coming and death. According to Peter, they knew that Christ's death would provide a great deal for those who would live after His death:

> Concerning this salvation, the prophets, who spoke of the grace that was to come to you, searched intently and with the greatest care, trying to find out the time and circumstances to which the Spirit of Christ in them was pointing when he predicted the sufferings of Christ and the glories that would follow. It was revealed to them that they were not serving themselves but you, when they spoke of the things that have now been told you by those who have preached the gospel to you by the Holy Spirit sent from heaven. Even angels long to look into these things (1 Pet. 1:10,11).

As these holy men of God studied Isaiah's writings, they discovered that a complete transferral would take place through what Jesus would suffer. He took as His own everything that belonged to us (those in sin) and gave us everything that belonged to Him (a Man without sin).

Christ even embraced as His own the things life would serve to us: damnation, sickness, sorrow, guilt, loneliness and much more. He replaced these things with salvation, health, freedom from internal problems of stress, joy and fellowship, to name just a few of the benefits His suffering and death provided.

Everything Jesus went through had eternal purpose wrapped in it. Keeping this fact in mind, the Body of Christ should not just study the sufferings of Christ during Easter, and forget about His sufferings and His cross the remainder of the calendar year. We must seek to understand more fully Calvary and the divine plan God used to set us free from the sin that would lead us to an eternal hell.

New believers must be taught fully about this awesome plan of God's for all who repent of their sins and accept His Son. People join the family of God every day without a full understanding of what Christ went through so they could be accepted in the family. Those of us who have been in the family for a while should also remember what He did for us regularly, not just annually. Salvation is free for those who will repent and receive Christ into their lives as Lord, but it cost Him His life.

HIS DEATH LEADS TO LIFE!

These facts concerning His suffering are of great importance. However, we must not forget about the freedom His suffering also provided. In addition to new members needing to be taught about the Cross, they should also be taught about how special they are to God, who allowed His Son to experience such suffering for them.

....

Jesus died for us, but we must live for Him.

....

We must remember and teach others that Christ's suffering was not the end, but the *means* to an end! A great divine plan was hidden within the garden, and the Body of

Christ must learn the experience of the Cross and implement it throughout their lives. Jesus died for us, but we must live for Him.

As pure gold that is hidden within the earth, the sufferings of Christ have been hidden within a principle that, once found, will change any person, family, city or nation. Anything of great value should be searched for with a diligence that equals the value of the thing searched for. You would not search for a penny with the same diligence as you would search for a check for $1,000, unless the penny was a rare coin that was worth more than $1,000.

The wise man said, "It is the glory of God to conceal a matter; to search out a matter is the glory of kings" (Prov. 25:2). Many people spend years of their lives and a great amount of money trying to find hidden treasures or precious metals in the earth. They spend their time and money for a chance to be rich, although they have no guarantee.

Christians, however, do not have to take any chances when it comes to the provisions of Christ. We must be willing to search for what God has concealed within Christ's life, sufferings, death and resurrection.

"The kingdom of heaven is like treasure hidden in a field. When a man found it, he hid it again, and then in his joy went and sold all he had and bought that field" (Matt. 13:44).

As the prophets were told, we are the benefactors of this treasure. If the prophets predating Christ could find it, there is no doubt we can also find it, because it belongs to us.

Now, you may not know where to start looking for this treasure (principle) being discussed here. Thank God we do not have to search alone. The Spirit of God is with us and He has the maps leading to the treasure. Allow Him to lead and guide you, and your spiritual life will soon be filled with the riches and treasures from heaven. Jesus promised:

> "When he, the Spirit of truth, comes, he will guide you into all truth. He will not speak on his own; he will speak only what he hears, and he will tell you what is yet to come" (John 16:13).

I believe that the Spirit of God has revealed this prayer and identification principle to help us find the treasure.

THE P.U.S.H. THAT IS REQUIRED

Since I have begun to share this principle with the Body of Christ, some have stopped practicing it because of the cost of searching for this hidden treasure. Bishop Wellington Boone can help us here, through the P.U.S.H. principle he introduced us to in his book *Breaking Through*.

P.U.S.H. stands for "Pray Until Something Happens!" A woman in labor pains cannot stop pushing when the doctor or nurses report they can see the head of the baby. No, she is compelled to push all the way through until the birthing process is complete.

In contrast, sometimes it seems as though the Church has been pulled into the world's way of thinking in that we try to accomplish or hope to receive spiritual blessings instantly—without "pushing." There is no instant "just add water" blessing in the kingdom of God. Even when we think what has come into our lives came instantly, remember that someone had to suffer for it. His name is Jesus.

I believe that once the Body of Christ realizes how Isaiah 53 should be a part of our everyday lives, nothing can prevent us from "pushing" to see that others are delivered from their sins.

Even in our churches people are hurting and in sin from which they are unable to break free. Christ has finished the work, but many are still under the bondage of this world system and the enemy's illegal control. Could it be that their deliverance will come from those who love them enough to P.U.S.H., never growing weary of numbering themselves with them?

OUR LEGACY OF SUFFERING

Christians need to realize that we are heirs not only of the salvation Jesus won for us on the cross, but of the pattern of His suffering as well. Everything Christ did in His earthly ministry was meant for those who would follow His example. Those who name the name of Jesus must follow and model to the world what they have learned from Him. This includes His willingness to suffer and even to die on behalf of others.

> To this you were called, because Christ suffered for you, leaving you an example, that you should follow in his steps (1 Pet. 2:21).

The word "suffering" causes most of us to think about physical problems or things such as uncomfortable living conditions. We sometimes stop short of the full meaning of Christ's suffering because of the awful way this world treated Him physically. Certainly He suffered in the flesh, but before He did, He faced that time of suffering in the garden through prayer. This was the spiritual suffering that enabled Him to face the physical suffering. According to the apostle Peter, this is a pattern for us:

> Therefore, since Christ suffered in his body, arm yourselves also with the same attitude, because he who has suffered in his body is done with sin. As a result, he does not live the rest of his earthly life for evil human desires, but rather for the will of God (1 Pet. 4:1,2).

Listen also to the apostle Paul:

> We then that are strong ought to bear the infirmi-
> ties of the weak, and not to please ourselves. Let
> every one of us please his neighbour for his good to
> edification. For even Christ pleased not himself;
> but, as it is written, The reproaches of them that
> reproached thee fell on me (Rom. 15:1-3, *KJV*).

Some Christians today in some places are experiencing
persecution and physical suffering for the faith. I believe
there is an additional way to suffer that will free people
who are also suffering. We must be willing to bear their
infirmities and their spiritual suffering. This is the reason
we must understand how Jesus set us free through His suffering, and the example this sets for us.

The apostle Paul prayed to suffer like Jesus so that he
could know the Lord and the power that comes through
this kind of suffering:

> I want to know Christ and the power of his resur-
> rection and the fellowship of sharing in his suffer-
> ings, becoming like him in his death, and so, some-
> how, to attain to the resurrection from the dead
> (Phil. 3:10,11).

Today, many believers would love to perform the miracles Christ performed; some desire to command an audience the way He did; still others seek the knowledge and
wisdom He had in discipling others. However, how many
are seeking His sufferings the way the apostle Paul did?

Paul performed the miracles, commanded the crowds
and discipled men. His ministry included all those things
we so greatly desire, and yet Paul wanted the sufferings. He
realized that even though the works of ministry were and
are very important, that was not how Christ saved the

world from sin and destruction. He wanted the power that saved the world working in his life and ministry. Are we willing to yearn for this the way Paul desired?

GOD IS STILL IN CONTROL!

I believe that one reason Christians are reluctant to follow in Christ's footsteps of spiritual suffering for others is that, down deep, they think Satan is the cause of all suffering. Understandably, we do not want to come under the power of Satan.

It is extremely important, however, to realize that it was God, not Satan, who subjected Christ to His suffering on the cross; and that God will retain control over our own suffering on behalf of others.

All this is revealed in that key chapter, Isaiah 53. There we learn, "It was the Lord's will to crush him and cause him to suffer" (v. 10). It was not Satan but God the Father who caused Jesus to face this great season of suffering.

This agrees perfectly with the prayer Jesus prayed in the garden of Gethsemane to let the cup of suffering pass. *If someone else controlled the situation, why would Jesus pray to the Father to remove the cup?* Of course it is because He knew the Father was in control.

Some would try to explain Christ's suffering and death in terms of God's pulling His hand back and allowing the enemy to take the life of His Son. The truth is that any involvement the enemy may have had in Christ's suffering and death, God used to complete His plan—not only used, but also allowed.

In this entire event, the only time the enemy Satan is even referred to is when Christ releases Judas into his hands to betray Him.

"It is the one to whom I will give this piece of bread when I have dipped it in the dish." Then, dipping the piece of bread, he gave it to Judas Iscariot, son of Simon. As soon as Judas took the bread, Satan entered into him. "What you are about to do, do quickly," Jesus told him (John 13:26,27).

According to the Scriptures, Jesus' suffering for others was totally within the eternal plan of God. It was for this reason that Jesus came to earth. Christ even rebuked the apostle Peter for thinking otherwise:

> From that time on Jesus began to explain to his disciples that he must go to Jerusalem and suffer many things at the hands of the elders, chief priests and teachers of the law, and that he must be killed and on the third day be raised to life. Peter took him aside and began to rebuke him. "Never, Lord!" he said. "This shall never happen to you!" Jesus turned and said to Peter, "Get behind me, Satan! You are a stumbling block to me; you do not have in mind the things of God, but the things of men" (Matt. 16:21-23).

All this not only means that we should accept our role of suffering in the spirit as from God, but also that we can trust Him not to allow us to suffer more than we can bear. God, not Satan, is in control.

This is the reason Father God was "pleased" as He bruised His Son and our Lord (see Isa. 53:10, *KJV*)—because it was God who created and was unfolding the plan to win the souls of the people He created, but who had fallen away from Him.

Looking at Christ's suffering, many people today—and maybe even Satan himself—think that Satan is winning. How wrong they are! Despite Christ's suffering, and ours, victory is at hand! There is nothing anyone can do to stop it. By being numbered among the transgressors, willing to suffer as they suffer, we can be a part of that victory.

CHRIST AND THE PRAYER OF IDENTIFICATION

I was overwhelmed at the way this Numbered with the Transgressors principle was received when I presented it to students at the University of Virginia in Charlottesville, Virginia. In this meeting, white, black, Asian and Latino people were present. Most of the students were very intelligent, near or at the top of their class. They seemed to listen to me as though they were in one of their classes. You could hear a pin drop on the carpeted floor.

I noticed that no one cried or showed any kind of emotion, as in previous presentations. The thought ran through my mind that maybe the grace and anointing on this message had ended. Now, please do not think I believe crying is what determines God's presence. Previously, though, while I was speaking, the Holy Spirit would move and people would cry long before the suggested prayer time. We are creatures of habit and sometimes we forget that God is God and can do whatever He wills!

Still, after my presentation I gave these students the same instructions about how to pray by "numbering" themselves in attitude and compassion, and told them to begin. Suddenly it appeared as though the entire room had caught fire, set by the Holy Spirit. It seemed as though the entire time I was speaking the Spirit of God was pouring gasoline on everyone and the prayer time became the match. One woman told me later she had never experienced intercession that way. She was an experienced intercessor and minister whose life and words I could trust.

"TEACH US TO PRAY"

I believe this kind of response is due in part to the intensity of the idea of identifying with others in prayer. Jesus prayed this way all the time; and the Bible records that those close enough to Him to hear what and how He prayed asked Him to teach them to pray, too (see Luke 11:1).

Let me ask you: When was the last time someone asked you to teach him or her to pray? Prayers are offered regularly in churches all the time using great zeal and emotion. Yet these prayers are not causing many people to ask for instruction from those who are praying.

Many in the Church try to free themselves from answering this question by using the excuse that we simply do not pray as powerfully as Jesus did. Remember two important facts about Christ's earthly ministry, however. First of all, He came to the earth not as God, but as a man who was full of God's Spirit.

> But [he] made himself of no reputation, and took upon him the form of a servant, and was made in the likeness of men: And being found in fashion as a man, he humbled himself, and became obedient unto death, even the death of the cross (Phil. 2:7,8, *KJV*).

The fact is that we have humble, Spirit-filled servants today; but few seem to be seeking them so they can learn how to pray.

Second, remember that Jesus told the disciples they would do greater things in their earthly ministries than He did in His.

"Verily, verily I say unto you, He that believeth on me, the works that I do shall he do also; and greater works than these shall he do; because I go unto my Father" (John 14:12, *KJV*).

PRAYING AND IDENTIFYING

It is my belief that the disciples asked Christ to teach them to pray not only because He prayed a great deal, but also because of how He prayed and the intensity with which they heard Him praying. Using Isaiah 53:12 as our reference, it is my opinion that the disciples asked Him to teach them to pray because they heard Him as One who was truly numbered with the transgressors. He identified with them so powerfully that He prayed from the position of someone who needed freedom Himself.

This kind of prayer had to have puzzled Christ's disciples because they knew, better than anyone else, that Jesus was totally free from sin. They walked, slept and ate with Him; and not once did they witness a transgression. Yet He could pray as though He were a transgressor!

The disciples wanted Jesus to teach them to pray in this way because the effectiveness of such prayers was very apparent. People under demonic control, sick unto death, in the grips and acts of sin—even the dead—responded to Christ because of this form of prayer. These men witnessed this power over life's problems. When Christ faced these various situations, He spoke words of freedom and the person was delivered. If you remember, He rarely prayed in these situations because He had already prayed. All that was needed now was a pronouncement of freedom.

The private prayer life of Christ is recorded only a few

times in the Scriptures. Father God did not reveal what His Son prayed for during those intimate times. However, I believe the intensity and focus of Christ's prayer life can be found in the same place we learn of His sufferings—Isaiah 53.

PRAYING AND SUFFERING

At this point, the question could be asked, How does Christ's prayer time relate to the suffering He went through? Through the sufferings of Christ, I believe we get a closer look into His private prayer life. One of the few times Scripture shows the intensity with which Christ prayed was when He agonized in prayer in the garden of Gethsemane, just before He went to the cross.

As we reflect on this scene, it is important to note that Jesus was praying for Himself in His hour of need. Why? Because He had to drink from a cup that was full of sorrow, suffering and even death. Remember, He did not fill this cup Himself. We did with our sins. If we filled it, then we should have had to drink it; however, He drank our cup as we watched, as if watching a sideshow. For this reason, Isaiah's writings concerning Christ are very important to our understanding about this one major part of His private prayer life.

I do not believe Jesus changed His prayer life in Gethsemane. At this point in His life His prayers increased only in intensity because of the service He was about to perform for us and for Father God. Throughout His earthly ministry we find Jesus identifying with those in sin and distress.

For example, there was the time when Jesus was told about His friend Lazarus's sickness (see John 11:1-44). He told the messenger to return and tell Lazarus's sister that this sickness was not unto death. By the time the message arrived from Jesus, Lazarus was dead. Jesus then took His time getting to Lazarus. He told Martha that He was the resurrection and the life. Then Jesus sent for Martha's sister,

Mary, and the mourners at the house followed her to the burial site.

When they arrived at the tomb, the people were weeping intensely. The Bible tells us that Jesus wept, too. Yet He had already told the messenger that Lazarus's sickness was not unto death. Jesus fully knew what He was going to do at the burial site. In His prayer to Father God, He indicated that He had already prayed to Him about Lazarus (see John 11:41). Why then did He cry one tear if He knew His friend Lazarus would soon be standing there with Him? He was not crying for Lazarus, but *for the people experiencing sorrow because of sin's wages, death.* Jesus knew the Father would hear His prayer, but He so identified with the sorrow of Lazarus's friends and family that He wanted to allow them to experience that fact.

....

Jesus could pray effectively for people to be released from the grips of sin and death, because He had numbered Himself with them.

....

Because Jesus was numbered with the transgressors, just as Isaiah 53:12 predicted, no one had to explain to Him how Lazarus's loved ones felt; He would pray on target and with feeling. He knew firsthand how they felt. Jesus had no problem praying for people to be released from the grips of sin and death, because He was in the number with them. When we can feel through experience who and what needs prayer, it becomes easier to pray. When you are in the number, the victory or the answer desired is soon at hand.

CLAIMING PEOPLE FROM SATAN

People both inside and outside the Church need to experience the freedom we have found in Christ our Savior. Those outside the Church are being held illegally, because Christ's death, burial and resurrection set all people free. Satan has no rights at all to anyone born on earth! Even if they are born in a prison, they can freely use a key to walk free. They must, however, tell the prison guard (Satan) that the key has been provided and command that they be set free. Jesus will then walk up to the door and open it, surprising the person behind the bars for it was not even locked. All locked doors were opened more than 2,000 years ago!

The attitude of the Church sometimes suggests that those who have not acknowledged Christ still belong to Satan. They do not! Christ died for the entire world and, through His blood, paid the price for the soul of every person alive then and those who would ever be born. The apostle Paul wrote: "For ye are bought with a price: therefore glorify God in your body, and in your spirit, which are God's" (1 Cor. 6:20, *KJV*).

The reason Satan can keep control over many people is that they or the Church of Jesus Christ allows him. The Body of Christ must take the attitude that every person ought to belong to Jesus. We must determine to take the good news of freedom to them, loosing them from all chains that bind them and thereby hinder them from experiencing the life provided for them in the Kingdom. Jesus said:

> "Verily I say unto you, whatsoever ye shall bind on earth shall be bound in heaven: and whatsoever ye shall loose on earth shall be loosed in heaven" (Matt. 18:18, *KJV*).

You may ask, "What if those in bondage do not want to receive the life of Christ to enter the Kingdom?" God created us with the ability to choose whether we want to receive the love of God or not. Many people, however, have given Satan the right to enslave them, whether because they do not know any better or because they know better but love their sin, and are therefore slaves to sin; or because they have been blinded and deceived by Satan; or any combination of these reasons. For those who are resistant to the love of God for whatever reasons, we can use the weapon of prayer to cause things around them to change. These changes, whether good or bad, can serve to help prepare their hearts for the gospel.

Numbering ourselves with transgressors is an effective form of prayer that can win the hard cases. We must never release people into the hands of the enemy, even though it seems as though that is what they want. We must never give up even when it seems as though they cannot be won. I know they can be won through prayer.

Kevin McDaniel, a Christian musician at a presentation of the Numbered with the Transgressors principle, was convicted that he should stand in the number for his father, who had been a reprobate and womanizer for years. Kevin later wrote, saying:

> A spirit of intercession hit me and I actually became my father. I envisioned pornography. I tasted liquor in my mouth. I felt drugs. I felt the pain, the anguish, the ugliness, the sin. I felt guilty on the inside, then I began to pray. I remembered all of the times I had told him, "You need to get right." Now I understood why he couldn't. I was a high and mighty Christian, the authority figure, the one who said, "Let me pray for you because I can get through to God."

Only after this man had confessed that he, too, was a sinner, and agreed with his brother to pray for their father from "the number," not from a self-righteous position, did things with the father began to change. Not long after virtually *becoming* his father in prayers of identification, his dad called to ask if he could come home. He did, not only to the home of Kevin's brother Daryl, but to his heavenly Father's home as well.

IDENTIFYING AT THE TABLE

Eating a meal with someone else is an important event in eastern countries, and the same held true for the Jews in Jesus' day. To sit down and eat with someone was to share a type of covenant meal. This is why it was so upsetting to the religious leaders when Jesus saw Zacchaeus in the tree and told him He would eat at his house that day. None of the religious leaders would even set foot in this man's house because he was a tax collector. Yet Jesus had invited Himself to eat with this man who, in the eyes of many of the Jews, was the scum of the earth. This time of eating and fellowship indicates to us that Jesus identified with this man whom everyone else hated.

As we have seen, though, Jesus was a man "in the number." He also stayed in the number, never assuming an exalted position over the ones for whom He came. When He prayed, His prayer had to also be prayed from that position of being in the number. When you pray from the number, then you are able to maintain compassion for the ones for whom you are praying. Jesus was full of compassion, and He demonstrated it by eating a meal with Zacchaeus. He demonstrated it in praying for transgressors even when no one else around Him identified with them in this way.

4

BRINGING FORTH THROUGH TRAVAIL

Students from several colleges in the Raleigh, North Carolina, area inspired me by their receptiveness to this Numbered with the Transgressors principle.

The students, who were associated with the New Generation Campus Ministries founded by Bishop Wellington Boone, gathered at a hotel conference room. They were happy to see each other and were very excited about the service. It was my belief that God wanted me to share with this group the new prayer principle. After an energy-filled worship service, I began to share with these students.

While I was in the midst of sharing, the Holy Spirit moved in as He had done in Richmond, and cut the teaching short. After the principle was fully explained, the students began to pray for unsaved family members with the attitude that they needed to be set free from sin. The students began to pray and cry so loud that they could not hear me speaking to them through the PA system.

The only time I had witnessed anything like this kind of prayer intensity was in Seoul, Korea, at Dr. Yonggi Cho's church I had never seen it in this country This caused me to be a little alarmed because I was not sure how to handle what was happening. The prayer time by the people in Richmond was intense, but these students surpassed their intensity level. I stood up front, watching these people and not knowing what to do next. Then, in a whisper, I prayed, "Holy Spirit, please release your people." In an instant, as though everyone heard at the same time, the audience stopped praying with that intensity, but continued to cry softly. My heart was pleased to see that God's Spirit was continuing to back this message with His presence. All at once I understood what had taken place in the hearts of the students. *The Holy Spirit allowed them to feel the heart of Jesus for the lost.*

The students, through instruction, agreed to number themselves with their lost family members. By helping them understand the need of these loved ones, the Holy Spirit had numbered them with the transgressors.

This session taught me what I knew by experience but could not explain. The Holy Spirit is doing all the work through this kind of praying; He is only looking for willing vessels!

PRAYING WITH PASSION

The Holy Spirit has mobilized a tremendous amount of prayer in this decade for Kingdom efforts worldwide. As a result, people in the Body of Christ are praying for a wide range of subjects. Given this increase in the amount of prayer, many are still yearning for more intensity in their prayer time. My observation is that more people understand the importance of prayer, but prayer with a passion is, on the average, still lacking.

As we have seen, Isaiah's prediction of Messiah's suffering includes the fact that He would be "numbered with the transgressors." Let's investigate that account further to see what insight it might give into how to increase prayer intensity

In Isaiah 53:11, a new concept is introduced. The subject of "travail" is presented, specifically how Father God responded to His Son's travail:

He [God] shall see of the travail of his soul, and shall be satisfied: by his knowledge shall my righteous servant justify many; for he shall bear their iniquities *(KJV)*.

The Father was satisfied when He saw the travail of Jesus' soul. I have heard messages during the resurrection season that paint the picture of God turning His face from the suffering Christ. I do not believe Father God would turn away from the victory His hands had brought forth. This was the defeat of the enemy of the soul of man. This was heaven's triumph over a world of sin, death, hell and the grave. Jesus was the Person God sent to the earth to accomplish all this, both for His Father and for those caught in evil's grip. Surely God watched every moment!

I believe that the Father allowed the prophet Isaiah to use language such as "pleased" in verse 10 and "satisfied" in verse 11 to describe to us His emotional state during the time of His Son's death.

Remember that everything Jesus suffered was out of obedience to the Father's will. He was fulfilling the plan of God that was established before the foundation of the world: After humanity's first sin in the Garden of Eden God said to the serpent:

And I will put enmity between you and the woman, and between your offspring and hers; he will crush your head, and you will strike his heel (Gen. 3:15).

Jesus is that offspring (*KJV*, "seed") born of a woman to destroy the works of the devil and overthrow his authority. This great truth is behind Scripture's references to

Christ as the One who was in God's plan from before the beginning of time. For example, John's vision in the book of Revelation included the following fact:

> All inhabitants of the earth will worship the beast— all whose names have not been written in the book of life belonging to the Lamb that was slain from the creation of the world (Rev. 13:8).

Sin did not catch God off guard. He has always had a plan to save humanity. The entire Godhead was working together to accomplish for man what he couldn't accomplish for himself.

THE TRAVAIL OF BIRTH

Now, let's investigate further what was accomplished by Christ's travail in obedience to the Father. The word "travail" is usually associated with a woman giving birth and the intense pain that accompanies the birthing process (see John 16:21, *KJV*). The word "travail" also fittingly describes agonizing in prayer, as when a person is interceding intensely on behalf of another person or situation.

The Bible reveals Jesus' intense time of travail in prayer on the night Judas betrayed Him. In Gethsemane, His disciples slept while He was praying to keep His soul (mind, will and emotions) in line with Father God's plan and will.

The Gospels' record of Christ's experience in the garden give us an opportunity to see the travail He experienced to birth the entire world's population into the Kingdom.

> Jesus went out as usual to the Mount of Olives, and his disciples followed him. On reaching the place, he said to them, "Pray that you will not fall into temptation." He withdrew about a stone's throw beyond them, knelt down and prayed, "Father, if you

are willing, take this cup from me; yet not my will, but yours be done." An angel from heaven appeared to him and strengthened him. And being in anguish, he prayed more earnestly, and his sweat was like drops of blood falling to the ground (Luke 22:39-44).

This was such an intense time in the earthly ministry of Jesus that His Father sent angels to minister to Him during this travailing prayer. Remember that *God was satisfied once He saw His Son accomplishing His will by travailing in prayer.*

Are you satisfying the Father?

WHAT TRAVAILING PRAYER LOOKS LIKE

As I mentioned earlier, the word "travail" is a word associated with the pain a woman experiences giving birth. Women who decide to have natural childbirth experience intense pain. Christ's experience with the spiritual dimension of such pain is reflected in His shedding sweat that

....

Jesus called on divine strength to accomplish His work on the cross so that humanity could be set free from the power of sin. This took three hours of agonizing prayer in the garden!

....

was like blood. Mark's account of Christ's travailing prayer in the garden notes that Jesus told Peter, James and John that His soul was "overwhelmed with sorrow to the point of death" (Mark 14:34).

Jesus' words to the disciples concerning His emotional state of mind, and the fact that blood dripped from His body, fulfill the words of Isaiah 53:11 about Father God seeing the travail of His Son's soul. Jesus was praying to keep His soul in line with the plan and will of God. He called on divine strength to accomplish this first phase so that humanity could be set free from the power of sin. This took a total of three hours of agonizing pain in the garden! We can understand His travail: It was not a fun time for our Lord.

The event taking place in the garden was *prayer*, prayer so intense that Jesus felt He needed His disciples to help Him accomplish its end by watching and praying with Him. Because of their weakness, they fell asleep (see Luke 22:45,46). So Father God had to send angels to strengthen Jesus. This was true travailing prayer!

AN EXAMPLE FROM MARRIAGE

For many, travailing prayer may appear to be out of their reach. A natural example from my marriage helped me to be able to embrace this kind of prayer.

The Bible instructs me to love my wife as Christ loved the Church (see Eph. 5:25). Therefore, I am to model for my wife in our home and relationship how much Christ loves His bride, the Church. He loved the Church so much that He gave His life for it.

The Bible also instructs my wife to submit to me as unto the Lord in the same way the Church is subject to Christ (see Eph. 5:22-24). Therefore, my wife models for me in our home and relationship how the Church submits to Christ.

Because the Church is the Bride of Christ, I become His woman, even though I am fulfilling the function of a man on earth. Because, as a man, it is almost impossible for me to understand how to respond to Christ as a woman to her husband, I learn this from my wife. She teaches me to submit to Christ as she submits to me. Her submissiveness to me is not for me to take advantage of, but to learn from.

Once I was going to the neighborhood store to pick up a small item. The store was only five minutes by car from my home. As I started out the door, my wife asked if she could go with me. I resisted her request because of the short distance and reason for my trip. I explained that the store was only five minutes away. "I'm going to run in and run right out. Before you know it, I will be back home."

I left my wife standing in the kitchen, got into my car and headed to the store. Before I passed my house, the Holy Spirit rebuked me for my lack of sensitivity. He said, "She did not care how far you were going or what you were doing. She just wanted to be with you."

This helped me understand the way I should want to be with my Lord. I should not always want something when I come to Him; I should just want Him!

In fact, I have learned that almost everything my wife does or has to experience as a woman and wife, Christ requires of me. Thank God for godly women in the Body of Christ who know who they are and their purpose. Because the men in the Church have at times used their positions of authority to put women down or even to control them, it is quite possible that we may have missed the lessons Christ wants us to learn from marriage. Remember that even though some Christian marriages are poor models, causing confusion for those watching, yet they are models nonetheless.

CARRYING OTHERS TO "FULL TERM"

I am indebted to Bishop Boone for teaching me about various parallels between the marriage relationship and the Church as the Bride of Christ. As Christ's "woman," the Church conceives and bears spiritual children. Just as a wife conceives and carries her husband's child to full term, so the Church has to conceive and then carry to full term those who need to be born again, thus becoming children of God. However, where are the disciples who are willing to travail in the pangs of spiritual birth for lost souls? The prophet Jeremiah spoke of this need:

> This is what the Lord Almighty says: "Consider now! Call for the wailing women to come; send for the most skillful of them. Let them come quickly and wail over us till our eyes overflow with tears and water streams from our eyelids. The sound of wailing is heard from Zion."
>
> . . . Now, O women, hear the word of the Lord; open your ears to the words of his mouth. Teach your daughters how to wail; teach one another a lament (Jer. 9:17-20).

The question is: How does the Church conceive? It is my belief that the Bride of Christ, who is the Church, conceives through her ears! That is, she gives birth to the visions sown into her heart by the Word of God, then delivers lost souls into the kingdom of Christ. The apostle Paul says, "Faith comes from hearing the message, and the message is heard through the word of Christ" (Rom. 10:17). The apostle Peter says that the message, the Word of God, is the seed that results in the new birth: "For you have been born again, not of perishable seed, but of imperishable, through the living and enduring word of God" (1 Pet. 1:23).

When the angel Gabriel came to Mary, the mother of our Lord, he told her she would conceive a child by the Holy Ghost. There was no physical contact between Mary and the angel. She was a virgin and no man had ever touched her. "And Mary said, Behold the handmaid of the Lord; be it unto me *according to thy word*" (Luke 1:38, *KJV*, emphasis mine). In other words, Mary received the word spoken to her and conceived our Lord.

Just so, the Church conceives through the ears and births through the mouth, in the form of the spoken Word:

"The word is near you; it is in your mouth and in your heart," that is, the word of faith we are proclaiming: That if you confess with your mouth, "Jesus is Lord," and believe in your heart that God raised him from the dead, you will be saved. For it is with your heart that you believe and are justified, and it is with your mouth that you confess and are saved (Rom. 10:8-10).

By God's grace the "seed," the Word, has been planted in our hearts. At the right time we must speak forth what the Lord has spoken to our hearts. This confession allows everyone to know that God is the Father of that new creation they can see in us.

Both natural women and the Church must carry the child of their husbands to term. The main difference between the two is that there is no pain killer for the Church. She must travail to bring forth seed unto God.

Most people in the Church seem to want to delegate this responsibility to a few chosen people, often called intercessors, to let them bear the burden of travail. I can find a separate ministry or a calling called "intercession" only one place in the Bible; and that belongs to Christ!

Wherefore he is able also to save them to the uttermost that come unto God by him, seeing he ever liveth to make intercession for them (Heb. 7:25, *KJV*).

Because Christ is our intercessor, no single person can claim intercession as an exclusive ministry or calling. Rather, the entire Church, as the Body of Christ, is called into the ministry of intercession. The Church is one with Christ and must do what He is doing. I believe we have lost some battles because we have the attitude that a few can intercede through prayer for us and for those who are lost. When a woman has a child, every part of her body is involved in the birthing process. So it must be with the Church.

The efforts supporting the "10/40 Window" during the last three years are an ongoing example of the power and ability of the Church when she joins together to pray for the same thing at the same time. A vast number of people unreached with the gospel live between the latitudes of 10 and 40 degrees north of the equator. Muslims in north Africa, and millions of people in India and Asia are included in this "window" of opportunity. In the North Carolina area where I pastor, local pastors join together under a banner called Unified 2000 to pray together for this great missions need and opportunity. The results have been tremendous.

The revival taking place in Argentina is also the result of pastors and the Body of Christ coming together to pray consistently. What a mighty force when the Church on earth, the nation, state or city comes together for a cause!

HAVE WE DESENSITIZED THE BIRTHING?

Women understand the travail of birthing; and sometimes they can transfer this natural knowledge to spiritual knowledge and bring forth unto the Lord. I believe this is why there are more women intercessors than men who intercede.

Some women who give birth to a child experience great pain and labor, but after the child is born they soon forget the pain. The child's birth brings great joy to her heart and life! During the birthing process, the father of the child is concerned about his wife, yet satisfied with her travail because by her pain he understands that the baby is near to being born. As a man, the birthing process helps me get an up-close view of how to travail to bring forth for my Lord.

Some women reading this book may have little knowledge about birth pangs because they took advantage of an "epidural" when they delivered a child. In this procedure, an anesthetic is injected in the area near the woman's lower spine. This numbs the lower body and allows the woman to remain alert during childbirth while blocking the pain of childbirth. An epidural often enables a woman giving birth to communicate with those in her room, or she may just fall asleep.

In such cases, the only way to determine whether the woman is having a contraction (birth pain) is by the readings on a monitor that is also attached to her body. This monitoring device shows electrical pulses that indicate the level of intensity of each contraction and the amount of time between them. A sharp spike on the monitor's screen indicates a very intense contraction. Although there will still be pressure as the infant exits the birth canal, the mother is not in as much travail as those who choose "natural" childbirth. I thank God my wife did not have to experience great pain during the birthing of our children.

However, the spiritual parallel to this procedure has a down side. Christ's woman, the Church, also seems to have chosen to have an "epidural." That is, she is losing her understanding of the kind of birth pangs and travail that will bring forth new children of God. Along with a reduction in the number of women who experience the travail of birth has also come a reduction in the number of people who are willing to travail for the birthing of lost souls. We need to understand that at times the Holy Spirit has to bring both men and women to new life through travailing in the spirit and with prayer.

A sister in Christ, Judith Benefiel, who copastors with her husband the Church on the Rock in Oklahoma City, had a dream that vividly illustrates what I am saying. The dream occurred after a service in which I taught about the importance of travailing intensely in prayer for others.

A woman at church had unintentionally said something that hurt Judith's feelings. She wept all the way home. That night she dreamed she was in a hospital surgery room waiting to donate an organ to someone whose life depended on it. Yet the patient who needed the organ was late—and when she did arrive she had a flippant attitude and expressed no appreciation for the fact that someone had volunteered to donate an organ that would save her life. Judith wrote these lines to me:

> The surgeon came toward me with a knife and I said, "Wait! Don't I get any anesthetic first?" He said, "I'm sorry, there is no anesthetic for *this!*"
>
> Then the Lord spoke in my sleep and said, "Judith, when you lay down your life for someone else, there will be pain. You must continue to travail till Jesus is formed in them." He let me know that if I go through life trying to protect *myself,* I might avoid some of the hurts in life, but I would never reach the highest joy of fulfilling my destiny and helping others reach theirs.

Judith added some appropriate lines from her experience giving birth to their third child. She said that when she was ready to deliver, the doctor discovered the baby was very large, and Judith was carrying it too high. For these reasons, the doctor would not give her any pain medication because he was concerned that it would slow down her labor and make delivery more difficult. Instead, he gave Judith medicine to make her contractions even harder, to force the baby down for birth. Painful as the birth was, it proved to be best for all concerned.

Judith saw a spiritual parallel to this experience. In a letter to me she wrote that praying in travail is sometimes necessary when we think the vision God has given is "too big" and "too high."

"Travail is uncomfortable and inconvenient to our flesh," she wrote, "but if we will refuse the anesthetic, which is protecting ourselves, God will see to it that we give birth to the greatest spiritual awakening this world has ever known."

THE PROBLEM OF GRADUALISM

How did the Church lose its sensitivity? I believe the enemy, Satan, slipped an epidural called "gradualism" into the back of the Church when it was not watching.

A parable about a frog dropped into a pan of water can help us understand how this could have taken place. If a frog is placed in a pan of hot water, it will immediately jump out. However, if the frog is placed in the warm water and the heat under the pan is turned up slowly, it will just sit in the pan and cook to death.

Likewise, Satan has tried not to desensitize God's people all at once. He has brought forth his evil devices gradually, turning up the burner slowly until the Church has become more and more insensitive.

....

Even many Christians cannot enjoy a movie
unless it has spectacular action scenes, most
revolving around violence and crime.
Hollywood calls it special effects.
I call it an epidural!

....

To choose an example indirectly related to our topic, when the television program "I Dream of Jeannie" was first aired many years ago, the viewing public did not want her belly button showing. The program's producers at first required that Jeannie's pants come up over her belly button, but it would be casually revealed many times during the program. Now women are seen on commercials in their underclothes, and only a very few find this to be a problem. Those under the control of the enemy use the argument, "These are the '90s."

In the 1960s and early '70s, actors were not allowed to sleep together in the same bed even when playing the roles of husband and wife. They were viewed sleeping in twin beds for the purpose of not giving the appearance of sexual relationship. Today, actors playing the parts of single people are found in the same bed—and they are not just sleeping. This is taking place during prime-time viewing hours.

Meanwhile, crime has increased in the streets and on television. Even many Christians cannot enjoy a movie unless it has spectacular action scenes, most revolving around violence and crime. Hollywood calls it special effects. I call it an epidural!

Remember the monitor connected to the woman in the birthing room. Think of it as the television sets in our homes. We can see the pain in society, but we do not realize we must engage in travailing prayer to change it. Jesus said when we see these things and much more, this is just the beginning of sorrows.

Remember also that the more the woman pushes during childbirth, the sooner the pain stops. We referred in chapter 2 to the P.U.S.H. program. It is time for the Church to "push," travailing in labor for those who are lost. It is time for Christians to arm themselves with the same mind that enabled our Lord to suffer for others, and that prompted the apostle Paul to pray: "My little children, of whom I travail in birth again until Christ be formed in you" (Gal. 4:19, *KJV*).

This verse indicates Paul realized there was a problem, and he could do something about it through travail. As the Church, we must get into our birthing position—on our knees.

WARNING:
TRAVAILERS MUST BE CLEAN

Before people enter into this level of travail, they should examine their own lives carefully. The psalmist said those who harbor sin in their lives "travaileth with iniquity, and hast conceived mischief, and brought forth falsehood" (Ps. 7:14, *KJV*). This verse tells us that those who have sin in their lives *will* bring something to birth—but it will be mischief and falsehood rather than the new creation God desires.

Many people who hear about the principle of being Numbered with the Transgressors want to start immediately. Before moving into this level of prayer, however, you must check your life to make sure the thing you are travailing for isn't inside you. It is important to understand that if someone asks you for prayer in an area in which you have problems, you should not pretend you can help the person be delivered. You should lead the person to someone who can stand in the gap for him or her, someone who has no difficulties in the area of the prayer need.

One of the main iniquities within the Body of Christ is pride. Some have what I call the pride of prayer. This is the pride that comes when those spending a great deal of time in prayer begin to believe they are closer to God or have more insight into the things of God than others do. It is possible that such people are receiving revelation and understanding; but it is my experience that the closer people get to God the humbler they become.

For this reason, members of the intercessory prayer group at my church aren't given any special recognition other members don't have. We work to keep them "under cover," so that the prayer ministry isn't thought of as an elitist position.

Now, I love and respect those on the prayer team, and I recognize the tremendous good they do. Those who spend time in intercessory prayer, though, must never forget they are members in the total Body. No special seats are set aside for them.

The enemy of our souls is always on the prowl, seeking to devour through pride those who would destroy his plans through prayer. This is why Jesus said, "When you pray, go into your room, close the door and pray to your Father, who is unseen. Then your Father, who sees what is done in secret, will reward you" (Matt. 6:6).

I want the rewards the Father gives. How about you?

JUMPING OUT OF THE NUMBER

In the previous chapter, travailing prayer was presented. At first glance, this kind of prayer can appear to be very difficult.

This was driven home to me when I was speaking to a group of New Generation students at A & T State University in Greensboro, North Carolina. I became very concerned as the prayers became even more intense. One young man began to scream and tremble in terror while begging, "I don't want to go to hell! NO! NO! NO!"

Remembering what worked in Richmond and Raleigh when the people were crying with loud moans, I asked the Spirit of God, in a whisper, to please release the students. He did, in the same way!

After the meeting, I asked the young man who was screaming what had caused him to scream in that way. He told me that when he began to number himself with the family member he selected to pray for, it seemed as though hell opened and he felt himself slipping into it. The person he was praying for was his father, who often demonstrated a hard heart toward the gospel message.

This was the first time I was aware of someone receiving a vision in conjunction with the Numbered with the Transgressors prayer. As disturbing as the experience was at first, the young man had a new attitude toward the salvation of his father from that day on! He received Jesus' heart for his father by seeing his father's eternal state.

Could it be that much of the Church has forgotten there is a hell, and many of our loved ones are on their way to that terrible place separated from God? What would happen if all Christians would start praying for their family members with this kind of intensity? Would they be tempted to "jump from the number"?

STAYING CONNECTED

We have seen that Isaiah 53:12 indicates Jesus was willing to be numbered with the transgressors. He associated with and ate with those who were downtrodden and/or in sin. The religious leaders of His day could not believe He would allow people of this nature to come near Him.

Jesus accepted those who had the disease of leprosy, which was both a medical and a social problem. The rabbis and other religious people of the day would not even walk down the same street a leper had walked on. Jesus not only allowed a leper to approach Him, but He also touched the man whom others considered "unclean" (see Matt. 8:1-3).

Why would Jesus do something like this? Did He not know this was not acceptable behavior? Certainly He did; but He was willing to break with tradition in order to stay in the number. Jesus never placed Himself above those He came to help.

Likewise, members of the Body of Christ today must stay connected with those in need. Yet, in the modern age, it is very hard to find church leaders who intentionally spend time around people caught in the grips of sin. Even the laypeople in the church keep themselves as distant from hard-core sinners as possible.

Yes, we work with the lost, shop in the same stores

with them and live near them. However, spend time with them where they spend time? No way! An attitude in the Body of Christ seems to indicate these people may contaminate us. Or are we actually showing the world and all who would really investigate how spiritually weak we are?

Most of the people who came around Jesus were either changed or convicted. This was because Jesus Himself was willing to be a light shining in a dark place, just as He counseled us to be (see Matt. 5:14-16). Yet, today, what happens when a Christian finds another Christian in the marketplace? When it becomes apparent that a coworker is a Christian, these two "candles" spend their time around each other's light. They talk to each other about what is happening at their churches, take breaks and lunch together and praise God for finding each other.

Could it be that the Father allowed these two Christians to find each other so they could work together for those who are yet to acknowledge Christ as Savior? Could it be that their coming together should be for the purpose of planning who among the *non*-Christian workers they are going to win for the Kingdom through prayer and friendship? These two Christians could agree together for the good of everyone on the job.

Who would Jesus spend time with at your job, or invite to lunch? Remember Zacchaeus!

ASSOCIATION BY HABIT

One of our major problems is that we are creatures of habit. At church services, people sit in the same seats beside the same people week in and week out. Then, after the service, their conversation is with the same people each week.

Stop and take a good look at your life, taking notice of the amount of time you spend making new friends and acquaintances. Some people only wave at their neighbors from a distance when they could have been in the community for years. If it is this difficult to talk with those who are around us in a nonthreatening way, how will we reach those in need who are outside our circle of recognition?

Jesus did not come to the earth to *know* about us, but to *become* us. He came to experience firsthand everything we could ever experience. People could not honestly tell Jesus He did not know how they felt or that He did not understand what they were going through. However, people in the world often tell His Church the same thing.

People also accuse the Church of lacking love. Yes, I know that some of their claims are to excuse themselves from conviction. A great portion of the time they are right, though. Jesus was moved with compassion to help people out of the grips of sin and sickness caused because of sin. Jesus hated sin but loved the people. The church expresses to the world that we hold to the same attitude when, in fact, we demonstrate a different attitude—that of hating the sin *and* the person in the grips of the sin as well.

Now, don't put me in some political camp. I am telling you about a Kingdom principle that is above politics. Compassion has no race, color, gender or political party. It belongs to the kingdom of God! Compassion is God!

> Beloved, let us love one another: for love is of God; and every one that loveth is born of God, and knoweth God. He that loveth not knoweth not God; for God is love. In this was manifested the love of God toward us, because that God sent his only begotten Son into the world, that we might live through him. Herein is love, not that we loved God, but that he loved us, and sent his Son to be the propitiation for our sins (1 John 4:7-10, *KJV*).

 In Matthew 14, Jesus had withdrawn to a remote and lonely place to pray after hearing of the death of John the

Baptist. Crowds of people went out from the cities and found Him, interrupting His prayer time. Yet He was quick to make Himself available to them. He wanted hurting people to find Him.

Unfortunately, the modern Church is not so willing to be found by the very people who need it most. I refer to this as "jumping out of the number." Because it has become the pattern of the Church to separate itself from those who find themselves in sin, directly or indirectly, they tend to stand alone. It should not be that way with the Body of Christ, because we are to seek the lost.

ARE YOU A JUMPER?

Some reading this may think this jumping principle does not touch them. You would be surprised how often human nature jumps out of relationships and association when something goes wrong. Allow me to unfold some of the ways I have found people out of the number when they did not even know it.

JUMPING FROM THE FAMILY

Some people belong to the same family but do not want to identify with or be a part of other family members. This kind of division of the heart can result from a variety of situations. It is especially true that when someone in the family gets into difficulty, he or she is often left on the outside looking in. One thing that will never change, however, is the blood flowing through the body. It is family blood!

In my estimation, the worst cases are when the Christians in a family no longer associate with others in the same family. I have heard it said this way: "I cannot agree with the drinking, cursing and lifestyles of the family." So these people shun their family and spend their time around other Christians.

Could it be you are in the family to help every one of your family members come into a relationship with Jesus?

RACIAL "JUMPING"

In the black community, some people distance themselves in every way possible from black people who live in the inner cities of America. This is despite the fact that some of these "jumpers" came out of the inner city themselves. These people spend a great deal of time talking negatively about the problems in the black community in an attempt to make themselves look better in the eyes of those around them, especially white people.

Some blacks will try to assure their friends and associates that in no way are they like those "other" blacks. Despite all their efforts, the skin covering their body is still black. If it is happening in the black community, like it or not, if you are black, you are involved. You could live in the far countryside, but you are still connected by race.

In the white community, some whites try to distance themselves from such groups as the Ku Klux Klan, skinheads and other racist groups, trying to convince blacks in any way possible that in no way do they support or approve of the actions of these groups. They will talk with blacks about the friends they have who happen to be black, but they would never have a friend among such groups.

These people are trying as hard as possible to distance themselves from the negativity of those with whom they might be identified. Yet, like it or not, through the racial connection, they are in the number.

These are examples of people who are trying with all that is within them to jump out of the number. The problem with this approach is that it does not work. In no way can we distance ourselves from people of the same race, because we cannot change the color of our skin or theirs. It is equally impossible for a person to change what family he or she was born into because of a lack of contact or acknowledgment.

Where did this attitude of jumping out of the number come from? Why do we seek to distance ourselves from

....

> *The underlying root of jumping from the number is pride, and Satan is the father of pride.*

....

negative things that others might associate with us? It is my belief that this attitude has its roots in the devil's kingdom.

The underlying root of jumping is pride; and Satan is the father of pride. The jumper tries to look good or better than someone else in the eyes of those watching.

THE JUMPING CHURCH

The Church is also a great expert when it comes to jumping out of the number. Let me give you a couple of examples.

JUMPING FROM BAKKER AND SWAGGART

God gave the Body of Christ two awesome opportunities to show the world this principle of being numbered with the transgressors. The first was the fall of Jim Bakker; the other was the fall of Jimmy Swaggart.

In chapter 1, I admitted my own tendency to "jump" from being identified with these two men when they fell. In both instances, the Church also tried to distance itself as far away as possible. Others went a step further by becoming official representatives against these two brothers in the public media. They actually profited from Bakker and Swaggart's predicament! And those Christians who could not publicly attack them turned off their TV sets for a while, at the same time running them down at work with people outside the kingdom of God. All the weight of these tragedies was on the shoulders of these men and their families, along with a few friends who stood beside them.

The question could be asked, Did these men not bring these things upon themselves? The answer is yes. The problem was that despite understanding that these men were wrong and, in each case, needed help, the Church seemed ready to crucify them in order to put them out of their misery.

Although the job of correcting these men was left to those who were positioned over them and their ministries, many in the Body of Christ were quick to place themselves in the position of these men's overseers in private conversations. Self-appointed leadership! Many seemed to assume the role of a prophet pointing the finger of judgment at these sinners. After their sin was exposed, not by the Church but by the media, the entire Christian world became prophets like Nathan, ready to point the finger of blame. However, Nathan had the courage to confront David personally, and the prophetic authority to come to David before anyone knew what he had done.

> And Nathan said to David, Thou art the man. Thus saith the Lord God of Israel, I anointed thee king over Israel, and I delivered thee out of the hand of Saul; and I gave thee thy master's house, and thy master's wives into thy bosom, and gave thee the house of Israel and of Judah; and if that had been too little, I would, moreover, have given unto thee such and such things. Wherefore hast thou despised the commandment of the Lord, to do evil in his sight? thou hast killed Uriah the Hittite with the sword, and hast taken his wife to be thy wife, and hast slain him with the sword of the children of Ammon. Now therefore the sword shall never depart from thine house; because thou hast

despised me, and hast taken the wife of Uriah the Hittite to be thy wife. Thus saith the Lord, Behold, I will raise up evil against thee out of thine own house, and I will take thy wives before thine eyes, and give them unto thy neighbour, and he shall lie with thy wives in the sight of this sun. For thou didst it secretly: but I will do this thing before all Israel, and before the sun (2 Sam. 12:7-12, *KJV*).

JUMPING AWAY FROM PAT BOONE

Recently the Body of Christ was given another opportunity to stay in the number with the Pat Boone situation. Pat was to appear with a heavy-metal rock star on the MTV network. As a joke, Pat was all decked out in metal studs and black leather like a rock star, while the real rock star was supposed to dress in Pat Boone's trademark style, white shoes and all.

As it turned out, the joke fizzled because the rock star backed out, and Pat was left there looking like a heavy metal "dude." Well, it was plastered all over the news and Christians far and wide cried out that Pat had backslidden. The fact is, he was recasting some rock music in his own style—but few bothered to find out the facts and Pat was in hot water with many in the Body.

Paul Crouch of the Trinity Broadcasting Network (TBN) said his office was flooded with e-mail. Many people threatened to stop their support of the network if Pat's show wasn't taken off the air. TBN aired a special program with Pat, his pastor Jack Hayford and Paul, so Pat could tell his side of the story. Once again, it was quite apparent how the Church treats those who even appear to fall. In all these examples, the Church jumped out of the number.

Although I never did trash Brother Swaggart or his ministry, I should say again that I was as far outside of the number as anyone. Not until God revealed to me the significance of Isaiah 53 did I understand that I was outside the number, and how to stay in the number.

How does a person number himself with transgressors, and stay there, refusing to jump out? Chapter 6 will help you get in the number and stay there.

CHAPTER

6

HOW TO STAND
IN THE GAP

While speaking in Pastor Sergio Scataglini's church in La
Plata, Argentina, I witnessed firsthand how God can enable
people to stand between sinners and salvation—to become
numbered with the transgressors.

This was the first time I had spoken in a foreign country
using a translator. I did not really know how the message
would be received, or whether anything would be lost in
translation.

I spoke in the afternoon service, which started at 5:00 P.M.
While I was speaking, people throughout the congregation
were crying softly, when something that had never happened before took place. The Holy Spirit came upon me in
a very powerful way. That in itself was not strange, but at
the same time, Pastor Scataglini, who was translating the
message into Spanish, was also overcome. Both of us had
a hard time continuing. The people started to cry a little
louder.

We instructed the congregation to pray for an unsaved
loved one and, as usual, the prayer intensity increased.
This time we brought these people to the front after they
prayed, asking them to stand in the person's place for
whom they had just prayed. Then Sergio led them to pray

the sinner's prayer in the stead of the person for whom they had prayed.

It was similar to the way I often lead people to stand in the gap on behalf of loved ones who are ill. Although they are healthy themselves, they are pleading for the health of someone else. Likewise, those who responded in the La Plata service were not trying to become saved for the person they were praying for, because no one could ever do such a thing. However, they were acting in faith that the person being prayed for would stand as they were and repeat the sinner's prayer and be saved.

We saw immediate results at the evening service, when Michael Fletcher, my spiritual twin, spoke. At the end of the service, he made an altar call and about 15 to 20 people came forward to receive the Lord in their hearts. *One of the people who came forward was the mother of a man who had just stood for her and prayed for her in the afternoon service.* This man hugged my neck so tight it seemed to take my breath away. He was so happy that he had stood in the gap!

JESUS IN THE GAP

Verse 12, the last verse of Isaiah 53, was the verse that seemed to hit me right between the eyes as God began to instruct me about this subject. It depicts Christ standing in the gap between God and transgressors.

Like so many chapters in the Bible where the last verse or two reveals everything and deepens the principles set forth within the chapter, this verse follows the pattern. Several verses in this chapter had opened up in ways I had never seen. Verse 10 clearly states that Jesus' Father (God) put Him through all the suffering He faced. Verse 11 says that the Father was satisfied with the travail of His Son. The enemy and enemies of the Kingdom were only used to bring God's will and love to pass through Jesus' death.

Verse 12, however, indicates how Jesus was numbered with transgressors, bearing the sins of many to make intercession for the transgressors.

The word "transgressors" in the original is from the Hebrew word *pasha,* which means to break away (from a righteous authority); to rebel, trespass or transgress; to apostatize; or to be refractory, to quarrel or to be offended. The basic idea is an aggressive breach of a civil or religious relationship between two parties. In international political alliances, the word connotes the deliberate casting off of an allegiance—a conscious revolt.

Think about it for a minute. Jesus was numbered among people who had the attitude set forth by this definition. Yet He was not ashamed to stand in the gap for them!

To identify with a person or group of this sort is to become guilty by association even when you have not committed any sin personally. Jesus was the only person who ever lived after the fall of Adam who had the right to remain outside the number. Yet He stayed among the transgressors, the rebels, to make intercession for them.

In chapter 4, we discussed travailing in intercessory prayer as a woman travails in childbirth. The basic definition for intercession is "one who stands in the place of someone else, willing to be judged for that person." In Ezekiel 22:30, God states:

> "I looked for a man among them who would build up the wall and stand before me in the gap on behalf of the land so I would not have to destroy it, but I found none."

The intercessor is one who stands in the gap between the holy God and sinful man, asking for mercy and a relationship with God on his behalf. Isaiah 59:16 also brings out this thought:

And he [God] saw that there was no man, and he wondered that there was no intercessor: therefore his [God's] arm brought salvation unto him; and His righteousness, it sustained him *(KJV)*.

....

Moses was willing to pay the high price of identifying with sinners to stand in the gap between his people and a holy God.

....

This verse indicates that because God could not find a man who would take the position of intercessor, He became the intercessor Himself. Jesus, who is God from God, became the intercessor for humanity.

PAYING THE PRICE

To stand in the gap between sinners and a holy God, you must be willing to pay the price of identifying with transgressors. Let's be frank: Not many of us are willing to do this, because it is painful. We have adopted the mind-set of the world: I've got mine, and good luck to the rest.

This mind-set can be overcome if you will just take the first step and put yourself in a position for God to answer your prayer on behalf of others. Seeing results from your prayers will encourage you to pray more, and more consistently and fervently as you see God honoring your willingness to become a part of those for whom you are praying.

We can also learn to be numbered with the transgressors by recalling inspirational examples in Scripture of those who paid the price of identifying with others. You may think the Numbered with the Transgressors principle applies only to Jesus. But the Bible magnifies this principle throughout its pages

MOSES: "FORGIVE, OR BLOT ME OUT!"

In Exodus 32, we find the story of Moses before God on Mount Sinai receiving the Commandments. Down in the valley, the leaders and people of Israel convinced Aaron, Moses' brother, to fashion a golden calf as the god that brought them out of Egypt. As the people reveled in disgraceful worship of the idol, they became drunk and began having free sex with each other. In anger, God told Moses He would consume the people and make a new and great nation through him (Moses).

In Exodus 32:11-14, Moses became an intercessor on behalf of the nation. He spoke not so much for the nation, but for the name of God and His greatness. In His mercy, God turned from destroying the people. Subsequently, Moses went down the mountain, and after seeing firsthand what the people had done to come so close to experiencing the wrath of God, he dealt severely with the people for their sin. Then Moses went back to God as a man "in the number," standing as an intercessor on behalf of the nation of which he also was a part: "The next day Moses said to the people, 'You have committed a great sin. But now I will go up to the Lord; perhaps I can make atonement for your sin'" (Exod. 32:30).

The next verse clearly shows that Moses knew who sinned. "So Moses went back to the Lord and said, 'Oh, what a great sin these people have committed! They have made themselves gods of gold'" (v. 31).

Now look at how Moses was willing to pay the high price of identifying with his people: "But now, please forgive their sin—but if not, then blot me out of the book you have written" (v. 32).

Wait a minute! Moses did not do anything wrong. He was on the mountain with the Lord. Why would he risk separation from God for what other people had done? Because Moses understood that he was a part of Israel, and that if Israel would be judged, then he should be.

Moses prayed from the position of "the number." He was not a jumper.

DANIEL: "WE HAVE SINNED"

The young Hebrew man Daniel is another instructive example. In Daniel 9, we find Daniel in Babylonian captivity. He was reading the words of Jeremiah the prophet, who wrote that the Lord would accomplish 70 years of desolation in Jerusalem. Now, remember that when Daniel read this he was in captivity; but it was written before he was even born.

Let's look closer at what Daniel found in the book. Jeremiah 25:11,12 and Jeremiah 29:10 indicate that God would end the desolation of His people, including their captivity, in 70 years. After reading this and understanding that the time was at hand to end the desolation, Daniel set his face to seek the Lord. He began to pray a revealing prayer. He prayed:

> "We have sinned and done wrong. We have been wicked and have rebelled; we have turned away from your commands and laws. We have not listened to your servants the prophets, who spoke in your name to our kings, our princes and our fathers, and to all the people of the land" (Dan. 9:5,6).

Allow me to come to Daniel's defense. This is the young man who would not eat from the king's table so as not to defile himself. The Bible says:

> Then the presidents and princes sought to find occasion against Daniel concerning the kingdom; but they could find none occasion nor fault; forasmuch as he was faithful, neither was there any error or fault found in him (Dan. 6:4, *KJV*).

Daniel would not submit to the royal statute of King Darius not to pray to God for 30 days, but to come and ask of him. Yet Daniel prayed at his window so that all could hear him. Therefore, it seemed somewhat strange for Daniel to pray, "*We* have sinned." We might think a better prayer might have been, "*They*" have done this and that. However, Daniel was praying from within the number, numbering himself with those who had transgressed years before he was born.

Was God pleased with Daniel's prayer of numbering himself with his nation's sins? Let's read on:

> While I was speaking and praying, confessing my sin and the sin of my people Israel and making my request to the Lord my God for his holy hill—while I was still in prayer, Gabriel, the man I had seen in the earlier vision, came to me in swift flight about the time of the evening sacrifice (Dan. 9:20,21).

Then Gabriel showed divine approval of Daniel's prayer by giving him understanding concerning the 70 weeks, which I believe is the time we are now living in. God looked with favor on Daniel because he was willing to stand in the gap for sinful Israel.

PAUL: "I COULD WISH MYSELF ACCURSED"

Now let's go to the New Testament and look in the book of Romans, where the apostle Paul is found to be standing in the gap.

From the time of his conversion on the Damascus road, where he first encountered Christ Jesus and temporarily lost his eyesight in the process, Paul was a man on fire for God. After Ananias came to him and laid hands on him that his eyesight might be restored, Paul became a new man, to say the least. Although he was sent to preach the gospel to the Gentiles, Paul never stopped being a Jew. He loved the Jewish people—and never jumped out of the number. He wrote:

I say the truth in Christ, I lie not, my conscience also bearing me witness in the Holy Ghost, That I have great heaviness and continual sorrow in my heart. For I could wish that myself were **accursed** from Christ for my brethren, my kinsmen according to the flesh (Rom. 9:1-3, *KJV*).

Paul was so much in the number that he wished his going to hell would send every one of his fellow Israelites to heaven!

Time and again, Scripture shows people of God being willing to stand in the number. Righteous Nehemiah prayed, "I confess the sins we Israelites, including myself and my father's house, have committed against you" (Neh. 1:6). At the same time, the faithful priest Ezra stood in the gap by confessing, weeping and throwing himself down before God and sinful Israel (see Ezra 10:1).

CHRIST, OUR SUPREME EXAMPLE

There is no better example of standing in the gap than our Lord Jesus Christ. He took everything belonging to us (sinfulness), and in return gave us everything that belongs to Him (righteousness). Jesus stayed in the number for the purpose of transferring our sins to Himself, and interceding for us with Father God.

Isaiah 53 predicts this role. Speaking as though Messiah's intercession had already occurred, the prophet stated that Messiah (1) bore our griefs and (2) carried our sorrows (see v. 4). He was (3) wounded for our transgressions, He was (4) bruised for our iniquities, He was (5) chastised for our peace, and He was (6) beaten, leaving stripes on His back for our healing (see v. 5). He was oppressed, afflicted, denied a fair trial, cut off from the land of the living and buried with the wicked. All of this because He numbered Himself with you and me.

In fulfillment of such prophecies, Jesus came and took on the flesh of humans to stand with them in the gap. Just before dying on the cross, He took the cup at the table with His disciples and said, "This is my blood of the covenant, which is poured out for many for the forgiveness of sins" (Matt. 26:28). Finally, in awesome fulfillment of Isaiah 53:12, Jesus specifically said, "It is written: 'And he was numbered with the transgressors'" (Luke 22:37).

Remember that although only Jesus' suffering, not ours, is effective for atoning for sins, He said: "I have set you an example that you should do as I have done for you" (John 13:15).

7

STAYING IN THE NUMBER

Dr. C. Peter Wagner, a well-known author about prayer and church growth as well as the founder of Global Harvest Ministries, invited me to speak at the International Conference on Prayer and Spiritual Warfare in Virginia Beach, Virginia. After hearing my message at New Life Church in Colorado Springs, where he and his wife, Doris, are members, Dr. Wagner asked me to share the Numbered with the Transgressors principle at the Virginia Beach conference.

While sharing the message, the Holy Ghost moved on people throughout the congregation. At the end of the service, I asked everyone to identify with someone unsaved and pray from that place of intercession. The Holy Spirit swept through the meeting in a mighty way. Once I came off the platform and went back to my seat, the spirit of intercession came over me and I went into a time of travail—so much so that I had to be carried back to my room.

The next day a man came to me, thanked me for the message and told me that he had numbered himself with his nephew, who was being rebellious toward his mother. That night, while we were praying, his sister led her son, this man's nephew, to Jesus. Praise God for answered prayer!

Dutch Sheets, senior pastor of Springs Harvest Fellowship in Colorado Springs, who was serving as the conference pastor, opened the meeting the next morning by sharing with us the testimony of one who had numbered himself with a man who professed to be an atheist. The night we were in prayer while the atheist was in a session with a counselor, the counselor was able to lead him to receive the Lord! Even the tough cases can be touched through this principle of prayer.

"Jumping" Began in the Garden

The trouble is that too many of us lack the "stick-to-itiveness" to remain in the number. As we have seen, even when a person comes into the understanding of praying in the number, the pain of travail makes it tempting to jump out. Human nature has a built-in jumper switch that we must always keep turned off. This tendency originated in the Garden of Eden with the Fall, when Adam tried to avoid responsibility for partaking of the forbidden fruit. "It was the woman You gave me," he told the Lord. Eve, in turn, said it was the serpent's fault. No one took personal responsibility, much less for anyone else.

Having five children, I have seen this tendency over the years when something wrong happened. Those involved would immediately start to point fingers at one another. As parents, my wife, Joanndra, and I never sat down and taught them how to pass the blame. It was in them from birth.

Not until my time of retreat, described in the introduction, did I realize I was a jumper, too. When my understanding opened up, however, I no longer wanted to live in Christ that way. I wanted to be like my Lord and Savior Jesus Christ and the other people of God in the Bible who stayed in the number. All of them achieved greatness for the Father and advanced the Kingdom by being willing to be counted among the transgressors.

I have recounted the conversation I had with my coworkers about Jimmy Swaggart. During the time of retreat, which became a time of intense study, it became very apparent to me that everything I had said in the lunchroom that day was outside of the number. My mind also went back to the television and radio interviews I watched and listened to. It was apparent these people also were outside of the number. The Holy Spirit helped me understand that Isaiah 53:12 meant that Christ Jesus would never have said to the people what I had said. Nor would He have been on television or radio discussing Kingdom business with people from another kingdom.

DEFENDING INSTEAD OF REPENTING

Now, you may be asking yourself, *What was so wrong about what I said? Shouldn't church leaders speak to the problems in the Church so the world will not have the wrong slant on them?* Well, let us review what other church leaders and I did wrong.

First, we tried to defend the Church. However, no one gave us that job! Christ can take care of His Church much better than we could ever hope to. The Scripture says:

Husbands, love your wives, just as Christ loved the church and gave himself up for her to make her holy, cleansing her by the washing with water through the word, and to present her to himself as a radiant church, without stain or wrinkle or any other blemish, but holy and blameless (Eph. 5:25-27).

This Scripture verse instructs us that Christ has and always will take care of His Church! He was the One, not I, who died for the Church, which proves that His love is greater than mine.

In the second place, I and many others who spoke to the issue of Brother Bakker and Brother Swaggart defended God. Yet I know that God has never asked me to take care of Him. He said through the psalmist, "If I were hungry I would not tell you, for the world is mine, and all that is in it" (Ps. 50:12).

God does not need to be defended! He is the all-powerful One. He is above all and is never caught off guard. In most cases, He is the One who reveals the sin of humans so they will repent. Bishop Wellington Boone says it this way: "Man will move by revelation or he will move by tribulation. God is after restoration, even if it causes man temporary problems."

What I was really doing was jumping out of the number! I did not want anyone to think I might have any association with these brothers' problems. I also wanted people to think of me as a good Christian in a good church. However, the truth of the matter is, simultaneously, I was showing them that I was a poor Christian, a part of the number who think we show our own strength and goodness by turning away from those in sin. Actually, all this does is reveal that the Church is too weak to take care of our wounded.

Now I understand that it takes the strength of God to be like Christ. In Isaiah 53:1 the prophet asked, "To whom has the arm of the Lord been revealed?" The answer lies in those powerful verses that follow, describing God's Servant, Messiah, suffering for others. This implies that the arm of the Lord, God's strength, will be experienced by those who walk in the footsteps of Christ. If we refuse to walk as He walked, then there is no need for the Father to give us His strength.

The people in the lunchroom at my workplace were ready for a demonstration of godly strength. However, the only way this could have happened would have been because I was willing to walk in the footsteps of Christ.

WHAT SHOULD I HAVE DONE?

I should have repented for the sins my brothers were found in as though I were the one found in it. I should have asked those people to forgive me and the Church for causing God's name and Christ's Church to be thought of in ways other than it should have been. I should have explained to them that, according to the Scriptures, the sins of these brothers reflect on the entire Church.

In no way do I make excuses for sin, but I can never fall out of love because of it. First Peter 4:8 states: "Above all, love each other deeply, because love covers over a multitude of sins." Because I did not stay in the number, however, the people in the lunchroom confronting me with questions about these public sins were denied the privilege of witnessing the Lord's arm of strength.

THE PRINCIPLE OF CORPORATE SIN

You may be asking, Why should we repent for the sin someone else commits in the Church? The answer is that Christians are one Body. If one part of your body, such as your eyes, commits sin by looking upon that which they should not, which part of your body can claim that it had nothing to do with that sin? If one part of your body is in sin, then the whole thing is in sin. Because Brother Swaggart, a man of God, was and still is a part of the Body of Christ, his sin affected the corporate Body of Christ, in effect infecting it with sin also.

The apostle Paul illustrated this principle by using a very graphic illustration:

> Do you not know that your bodies are members of Christ himself? Shall I then take the members of Christ and unite them with a prostitute? Never! Do you not know that he who unites himself with a prostitute is one with her in body? (1 Cor. 6:15).

So for the Body of Christ to cut a person off because he has sinned would mean a type of disembodiment!

HOW IT SHOULD HAVE BEEN

What a powerful example it would have been if, across the United States and the world, the television and radio had been full of Christian leaders repenting with those whose sins had been made so public. All the media and wolves in sheep's clothing who came after his flesh to eat him alive would have had to deal with the Body of Christ. Instead, we left him out there all alone and watched the wolves rip into him.

Musk oxen, which are part of the deer family, understand how to fight as a unit and protect their wounded. When attacked by an enemy, the entire herd lines up back to back, forming a circle of protection around all the female and baby oxen.

....

The Body of Christ should pray for and protect those whom Satan has crippled, either physically or spiritually.

....

One of the bulls then goes out to fight against the enemy until he becomes either tired or wounded. He then retreats back to the circle, where he is allowed to enter into the center of the circle with the females and babies. Another bull then goes out to confront the enemy. This will continue until the enemy is defeated or retreats from the herd.

The Church should have adopted this tactic, both individually and corporately, protecting those who had fallen from being attacked any further and bandaging their open wounds through love. We could have been a part of the goodness of God, which the Bible says leads men to repentance. Support letters should have come from Christians around the world—not just letters from people requesting their money be returned from donations given, in most cases, years prior.

We should listen to and follow the instructions of those who are working with the sinful people to bring healing. We must not try to restore a person faster than recommended by those who are working firsthand with the person. The full healing process must have an opportunity to work.

The Body should pray for and protect those Satan has crippled, either physically or spiritually. As James said:

> Is any one of you sick? He should call the elders of the church to pray over him and anoint him with oil in the name of the Lord. And the prayer offered in faith will make the sick person well; the Lord will raise him up. If he has sinned, he will be forgiven. Therefore confess your sins to each other and pray for each other so that you may be healed. The prayer of a righteous man is powerful and effective (5:14-16).

Once I realized my shortcomings in this regard, once I became willing to stand in the number, I am thankful to say that God used me in just this way. I can take no personal credit, but give all the praise to the Lord for the healing of a woman in Washington, D.C., the older sister of a good friend and brother in Christ, Pastor Olden Thornton.

The sister, Brenda Thornton, was seriously ill, even at the point of death. Pastor Thornton called me and solicited my prayers. I asked him to meet me in Richmond, Virginia, and to drive with me to his sister's home in Washington. The Spirit moved me to fast and pray all night in her home.

The next day, we went to the intensive care unit at the hospital where she was being treated. She lay unconscious in the hospital bed, and remained in that state even as I laid hands on her and prayed for her healing.

The very next day, however, Brother Thornton reported that his sister became, literally, a walking miracle. The doctors were astounded.

Why could I have not stayed in the number like that and travailed for the forgiveness of my brothers Jim Bakker and Jimmy Swaggart? If the Church had positioned itself in such a way as to cover our brothers with the love of Christ and stood with them in their time of weakness, then the world would have known that we are Christ's disciples. For "by this all men will know that you are my disciples, if you love one another" (John 13:35).

Heal the Person, Heal the Body

When the Body of Christ is positioned in this manner, intercession can be made not only for the individual sinner, but also for the entire church in the area of the individual's need. Just as the sin of a brother in the public eye affects the entire Body, so his healing can spread throughout the Body if we follow God's directions.

In Brother Swaggart's case, the need was freedom from the vice of lust. Years later, men and women in the Body are still dealing with this enemy of lust. Most of these people cover up this problem because of the way the Church handled those leaders. The lust problem still is not resolved.

Jim Bakker was the first national church leader to fall in a way that the entire Church and secular worlds could view and, at the same time, form opinions about the Church and its leaders. During this time, there were many reports and media forums concerning this matter. I think God was watching His Church to see how we would handle something of this magnitude. He knew what we would do, but He wanted the Church to know for itself.

The sins here included deception and perhaps greed. Are we so naive as to think other members of the Body aren't affected by these sins as well? Instead of the Body repenting with Bakker, many leaders played to the cameras, trying to make themselves appear above being susceptible to Jim Bakker's sins. Former supporters of his ministry treated the work he was doing for the Kingdom as though every part of it was dirty, throwing the baby out with the bath water.

Again, to stay in the number, the Church should have allowed the church government this man was submitted to to work through his problems with him and to handle the whole matter. No interviews should have been granted; preaching against theme parks and buildings or even wealth should have never taken place. We should have been on our knees repenting for the sin found in the Church. Then the Church could also have partaken of God's mercy and forgiveness.

CONNECTEDNESS AS A LIFE POSITION

Staying connected must be our life position. The strong are told to bear the infirmities of those who are weak. Just as Jesus did, we must intercede from a connected position. The Bible tells us that a little leaven leavens the entire lump. However, the yeast (leaven) cannot be on the outside of the bread. It must be worked into—connected with—the dough.

Keep this in mind when a church in your community is going through any kind of problem. Your job is to pray for that church and its leaders. Your job is not to go after the members and try to persuade them to become a part of your church. This is Jesus' church and His people. He can handle everything just fine.

Family problems, race relations and even citywide situations or problems also need someone willing to stay connected, someone who is a righteous seed to connect with it by staying in the number. You could be the one person in your family who will help the entire family come to the knowledge of Christ Jesus. If you act as though people having problems are from another planet, if you refuse to spend time with them or identify with them, how will they observe an example of Christ in you?

How often do we pray for members of our family? Although we no doubt lift our own needs to God frequently, are there some family members whose names we have not presented to Him at all?

TAKING THE CITY FOR CHRIST

The possibility of taking a city for Christ has recently become a goal of the Church. A great deal of spiritual warfare must take place to take our cities. Prayer—standing in the number—is one of the main weapons to use when attacking the enemies who are blinding the eyes and hindering the hearts of men and women.

From what place will you pray? I am not asking from what room or building, but rather from what position. Will you be praying from inside or outside of the number? It is my belief that Christians in general have stood afar off as we have prayed for the needy people around us. In doing so, we project the attitude that those people really need to get their lives together and live right.

Remember that God has us living where we do for a purpose. Perhaps you live where you do for the sake of your community and city. Because we live in the community and city, our approach to God is as a person who wants the best for the area. When crime and other ills of society take hold of the place where we live, we must stay in the number. Our prayer should include such words as, *our*, *we* and *I*. Words such as, *they*, *them* and *those* should be avoided.

As Christians, we come to the Father on behalf of the land, our land in which we live, or on behalf of the family, our family into which we were born. Staying in the number is the compassionate thing to do. Compassion in its fullest sense means saying, "That which is happening should not be happening. I am a part of what is happening, and, therefore, I will do something about it." Keeping that in mind, please carefully read the following Scripture reference:

> "If my people, who are called by my name, will humble themselves and pray and seek my face and turn from their wicked ways, then will I hear from heaven and will forgive their sin, and will heal their land" (2 Chron. 7:14).

This is one of the Church's favorite passages when revival is the subject. I believe our "wicked ways" also include all the wicked things taking place in our land. The passage says that God will come and heal our *land.* The Church also needs to be healed of its standoffish attitudes.

The Church needs to be freed from the attitude that causes it to disregard God's command to bear the infirmities of those who are weak because we think we are either better than or cannot relate to those in sin. To change this attitude, we will have to humble ourselves and become identified with the sin and problems of those with whom we have nothing in common, other than the fact that we are human beings living in this land.

People both within and without the Body are human and subject to sin. We may not have started the problem (remember Moses); we may not know who started the problem (remember Nehemiah); or we may not have even been born when the problem started (remember Daniel). However, none of these factors frees us from our obligation to do whatever is necessary to solve the problems.

If we have right thinking, we can seek the face of God, pray for change and God will move in ways we have not seen before. I believe this is the way the Church demonstrates that we are salt and light to the world. Stay in the number, and see the intensity of your prayers change and the answers to your prayers increase.

8

HOW TO PRAY WITHIN THE NUMBER

My wife, Joanndra, and her sister attended the International Conference on Prayer and Spiritual Warfare, where they heard a presentation of the Numbered with the Transgressors principle. They became convicted that they should pray for their older sister, who had not been in church for more than 20 years.

"We began to cry out to God for her salvation," my wife later wrote. "A couple of months later my older sister called me. During the course of our conversation, I asked her if she wanted to receive the Lord. She immediately said, 'Yes!' and I had the privilege of leading her to the Lord over the telephone."

LEARNING FROM THE LORD

What makes such intercessory prayer effective? How can we pray "within the number"?

In Luke 11, the disciples ask Jesus for instructions about how to pray. Christ began by teaching them what is commonly called the Lord's Prayer, a fuller form of which is found in

Matthew 6:9-13. All the necessary ingredients for an effective prayer life are found in this prayer or prayer form.

What I want to investigate further is the parable that follows this model prayer in Luke's account. This parable, in Luke 11:5-9, has a great deal to teach us about the kind of prayer we have been discussing throughout this book: "identificational intercession." The parable speaks directly to how we can "pray within the number." It is important that we closely review each verse for its underlying meaning, especially in terms of determining how it relates to those seeking to better understand or begin this kind of prayer ministry.

A Pilgrim in Need

Jesus' parable begins like this, quoting from the *King James Version* of Luke 11, beginning with verse 5:

> And he said unto them, Which of you shall have a friend, and shall go unto him at midnight, and say unto him, Friend, lend me three loaves; for a friend of mine in his journey is come to me, and I have nothing to set before him? (Luke 11:5,6).

Here we find a man telling a friend that a traveler has arrived at his house at a time when he was not expected—at midnight. For the sake of this discussion, let's say the journey the traveler is on represents a person's journey through life. Let us also say that the time, midnight, represents one of life's most difficult seasons.

We can further suppose that the person who is experiencing this difficulty comes to a Christian whom he not only knows, but also considers a friend. Sure enough, the man proves to be a friend because he is very happy to see the traveler, and welcomes him into his house even though the hour is late.

However, a problem becomes apparent soon after the traveler's arrival. The man has nothing to feed his friend because his cupboards are empty. For the sake of this example, the empty cupboards represent the fact that the friend has no answers for the traveler in the difficulty.

It could be that many of you have found yourselves in this situation and have tried to talk your way through it. When a person is tired, hungry or in great need, talk does not go very far. Unfortunately, however, we often use the difficult times others find themselves in to preach to them. In many cases, the person leaves still feeling empty and needy.

In my study of the witnessing techniques of the Early Church, I found they were quite different from ours. It seems they showed the love and power of God to those who did not know Jesus in order to introduce them to Him. Everyone was willing to listen to what they had to say once they met Christ in His love and power through them.

In those cases where we try to convince people everything will be okay, we may feel good about what we have said, yet deep down inside we know nothing was done to solve their problems or meet their needs. Those we witnessed to could have received Christ, the greatest answer of all, but they were still unskilled in knowing how to receive an answer to their need. Even if they receive Christ, we often go off to tell other Christians about what has happened.

Please do not misunderstand what I am saying. Leading a person to Christ is the greatest thing any Christian can do. Nevertheless, we should still help people with their needs because it was for that reason that they came to us initially. The question is, What should be done during these times?

We only need to follow the example of the man Christ taught about in the parable. This man did not try to help his friend with words only, but was determined to provide what he needed at the time he needed it. This caused him to leave his friend, the comfort of his home and his family (if he had one) and go to a neighbor-friend where he could receive help to supply the traveler's need.

For the sake of this example, we will say the neighbor from whom he was trying to get the loaves was God the Father. In this place there was enough provision for both himself and his friend. The householder knew the principle stated in Ephesians 3:20: "Now to him who is able to do immeasurably more than all we ask or imagine, according to his power that is at work within us."

THE PRINCIPLE OF PERSISTENCE
Now let us continue our study of the parable.

> And he from within shall answer and say, Trouble me not: the door is now shut, and my children are with me in bed; I cannot rise and give thee (Luke 11:7).

The householder seems to run into a brick wall. The one who has the supply does not immediately give him anything, even though they are friends and he recognizes his voice. Inside the house the man is at rest along with those he is responsible for, his children. The children are all safe with the one who has the supply.

Remember that for this example the person who has the supply represents God the Father, and the person standing outside the door represents a Christian who knows where the supply (answer) is. Yet sometimes when we go to the Father on behalf of another person, it seems as though He takes His time answering our request. We know He has the supply (answer), but nothing is happening.

I believe that in these times, God is bringing us into new understanding and compassion, into a position of being numbered with the ones for whom we are approaching Him.

Let us complete the text and discover what happened next.

I say unto you, Though he will not rise and give him, because he is his friend, yet because of his importunity he will rise and give him as many as he needeth (Luke 11:8).

This verse gives us the key that unlocks the principle we have been examining. Before we discuss this verse, I must ask you an important question. In the parable, who is hungry? Remember, when the traveler came to his friend's house at midnight nothing was set before him to eat. It is easy to see that he is hungry or has a need. However, I submit to you that *the man standing at the door disturbing his friend's rest is also hungry.* How did I come to that conclusion? By noting that the man would not allow the opposition to hinder him from getting the food. His neighbor finally came to his aid because of his "importunity." That word means *shameless persistence.* From the parable, it becomes very clear that this man would not be denied.

When a person is standing for someone else and is not being paid or has no personal interest at stake, opposition tends to cause that person to give up without a fight. This man wasn't like that. He was so persistent that it leads me to believe his own hunger must have been involved.

HUNGERING WITH THE HUNGRY

Here Christ is instructing His disciples in how this man embraced as his own the hunger of his friend he left back at his house waiting. If he had not personally identified with his hungry friend, he more than likely would have turned around at the slightest resistance and left offering an apology. However, he did not apologize; instead, he kept knocking on the door until he got what both he and his friend needed.

The waiting traveler could be anyone in need or in the grips of sin and unable to find a way out. In any case, such people sometimes come to Christians because they believe we can do something to help them out of whatever situations are troubling them. Sure enough, his friend returns with the bread and he can eat as much as his heart desires. Then he can rest from his journey having a full belly—or, as we have applied the parable, having received the answer to his problem.

....

To receive from Christ to give to others, we must become a part of their problem.

....

At this point, it would be easy to talk to this man about the friend who gave the bread. When people come to us for help or answers, we must remember that our cupboard is always empty. Yet we have a friend, Christ, with whom they may not be familiar, who has all the supply they need at any time. Nevertheless, to receive from Him to give to others, *we must become a part of their problem.* This enables us to pray with the intensity and shamelessness associated with the person in need.

It is important to remember that Christ will not give the children's bread to those outside the kingdom of God. If the man on his journey had gone directly to the house of the man who had the supply, he would not have had the confidence to keep asking because he had no relationship with him. The man who had the supply could have also called the authorities to remove the man at his door because he was a stranger.

The man who knew where to find the supply could not have given his friend directions to the house of the man who had the provisions in the hope that the man inside would get up and give it to him. He had to go himself!

Bear in mind, the man outside the door never introduced himself because the man inside the house knew him and his voice. This indicates the two men had a great deal of contact with one another. He approached him as though he had a right to ask for whatever he needed.

PRESENTING, NOT REPENTING

In looking back at Isaiah 53:11, we are told that the travail of Jesus justified many. Jesus' travail and death on our behalf provided for our freedom. He died for us as our substitute and *as us*, identifying with our need. In a sense, the man at the door became the substitute for the traveler he left at home. He identified with him in that he remained consistent before the one who had the supply.

We must remember when standing as this type of intercessor that Jesus is ultimately the only One who can bear burdens. Never can we repent for a person, because that is between that person and God. We can, however, *present* that person and his need for the Savior from a place of compassion, lifting up his needs with strong prayer and persistence.

At the end of the parable, the Lord encourages us by saying these words:

> And I say unto you, Ask, and it shall be given you; seek, and ye shall find; knock, and it shall be opened unto you. For every one that asketh receiveth; and he that seeketh findeth; and to him that knocketh it shall be opened (Luke 11:9,10, *KJV*).

Here the Lord is telling the disciples how to pray from the position of a child of God. The Father loves us so much that He did not spare His Son. What would He withhold from us now? Even when it appears as though nothing is happening, God has given this promise. If the children ask to change lives, communities or nations, He will do it!

RECEIVING ANSWERS

Luke also records a parable of Christ's that gives us insight into how fast the Father will answer the prayer of His children when they stay in His face waiting for an answer.

Then Jesus told his disciples a parable to show them that they should always pray and not give up. He said: "In a certain town there was a judge who neither feared God nor cared about men. And there was a widow in that town who kept coming to him with the plea, 'Grant me justice against my adversary.'

For some time he refused. But finally he said to himself, 'Even though I don't fear God or care about men, yet because this widow keeps bothering me, I will see that she gets justice, so that she won't eventually wear me out with her coming!'"

And the Lord said, "Listen to what the unjust judge says. And will not God bring about justice for his chosen ones, who cry out to him day and night? Will he keep putting them off? I tell you, he will see that they get justice, and quickly. However, when the Son of Man comes, will he find faith on the earth?" (Luke 18:1-8).

In this passage of Scripture, a needy widow pleads for justice before an unjust judge. At first he seems to be not at all moved by the woman's need and is in no way interested in helping her.

It is quite apparent to a person in need when a person has an attitude like this. Often, when a person finds herself in the shoes of this woman, she will keep her distance from others. However, this woman did not allow her attention to focus on that fact. Instead, she remained focused on her need, and on the fact that the person she was talking to could dispense the justice she sought.

In our case, we know that our Judge is just, and that our interests are at the center of His heart. The Father will avenge us speedily.

At the end of this parable, Christ asked His disciples an important question. Will He find faith on earth at His return? Having a mind-set to stand, to keep knocking and asking until we receive an answer requires faith, faith that says God, and only God, has the answer we need and we will not even attempt to go anywhere else for the answer.

Christ used the parables recorded in Luke 11 and 18 to teach the disciples about the importance of staying in prayer until they got the supply or answer they needed. In the first parable, the man was standing for someone else. Yet from the Kingdom position, when he became numbered with the one who came to him, he was really asking for himself.

In the second parable, the widow was standing for herself from the beginning, and she did not move until she received her answer. When the Father's children come to Him with a need and the attitude that He is the only One who can meet it, then the answer is going to come fast. When it does, it will be more than they can handle, even more than they asked for.

As the Body of Christ, we sometimes give up before we receive from God what we are praying for. If the problem is a very difficult one, we sometimes find Christians fainting all over the place. Don't faint; the answer is right at hand!

"GUMPING"

In his brief little letter, Jude writes:

> Keep yourselves in God's love as you wait for the mercy of our Lord Jesus Christ to bring you to eternal life. Be merciful to those who doubt; snatch others from the fire and save them; to others show mercy, mixed with fear—hating even the clothing stained by corrupted flesh (Jude 21-23).

From this Scripture reference, I have coined the term "Gumping." To explain what I mean by this term let us look at one of the scenes taken from the movie *Forrest*

Gump. I believe it clearly illustrates the parable of the importunate friend in Luke 11.

In one scene, while trying to rescue his friend Bubba, Forrest Gump saved the lives of several wounded soldiers who were trapped behind enemy lines. While bringing them to safety, he was shot in the buttocks. Yet at no time did he allow his own injury to stop him from helping others to safety. Unfortunately, Bubba, who was one of the last ones to be rescued, died shortly after he was rescued.

Forrest also saved a man who did not want to be saved. Captain Dan wanted either to be a war hero or to die in combat because all his relatives who had been in the army before him had died in battle. He lost both of his legs as a result of the enemy attack, and he blamed Forrest for saving him from death.

Just as he had not allowed personal injury to deter him, so neither did Forrest allow Captain Dan's attitude toward him to change how he viewed him. Instead, he stayed with Dan, embracing him until his attitude changed.

I say that "Gumping" is taking people out of harm's way when they cannot help themselves, despite any personal challenges we ourselves may be facing. When we move into intercession and carry those who cannot carry themselves, we are "Gumping." There will be those who do not want to be carried, but because of the compassion and example of God and Christ, we have no choice. Romans 5:8 states, "God demonstrates his own love for us in this: While we were still sinners, Christ died for us."

Christ, who went through much more than Forrest Gump, did it all to save us from hell's fire. We have taken on His nature and must walk as He walked. "To this you were called, because Christ suffered for you, leaving you an example, that you should follow in his steps" (1 Pet. 2:21). Like Forrest Gump, we must have the attitude that everyone we can help must be helped, even when we are in need ourselves.

TOUCHED BY INFIRMITIES

Allow me to share a testimony I received from Jack Munday, who is on the ministry staff of Promise Keepers. It is a moving witness to the power of placing ourselves in the number so that we are touched by the infirmities of those who are lost or in need in other ways.

In the midst of incredible growth of the Promise Keepers' (PK) Ministry through the Carolinas, Charlotte, North Carolina, was selected for a Men's Conference in June of 1966. Although I was on the PK staff, my wife and I were currently living in Greensboro, in a beautiful log home we built in 1983. Yet, to open the new PK office in Charlotte, the Lord was asking us to sell our home and move.

Realizing that we had moved 17 times in 26 years of marriage, we thought the log home would be our final "resting place." Nevertheless, the time came to put the house on the market. It was on a Saturday morning in early December of 1995 that the first interested family was scheduled to walk through our home.

That morning, my wife Bonnie was quiet I was planning to attend a PK Wake Up Call that evening ιṅ Greensboro, with Pastor Larry Jackson as guest speaker. Although the visitors were scheduled to come at 11:00 A.M., Bonnie left at 9:30 to go shopping—and didn't return until 2:00 P.M. I was worried. When she finally returned, I realized she was struggling about selling our home. Could it be that I misunderstood the Lord about the need to move to Charlotte? Bonnie and I have always had real unity in all our previous moves. What was I to think? I was confused as I left the house for the PK meeting.

Pastor Jackson spoke on intercessory prayer. He shared out of his own life how the Lord had allowed him to feel the sorrow and grief of others as he prayed. He said that "Only as we enter into their hurt and sense their pain can we identify with them, and pray more effectively for them."

In his closing remarks to nearly 300 men, he asked if there was anyone in our lives who needed prayer. He invited us to let the Lord help us to feel what they were feeling, and to share in their struggle. As Pastor Jackson led us in prayer, the entire sanctuary turned into a room of prayer, with weeping and sounds of groaning.

As I found myself prostrate before the Lord, I was praying for Bonnie. I really felt her sorrow and the struggle she had in knowing if it was God's will to sell our house, while still feeling the memories and emotional connection to our home. I was able to pray for her like I had never prayed before; and I will never forget it.

I couldn't wait to tell Bonnie all about our meeting the next morning, a Sunday. On our way to church, I started to tell about my experience when she stopped me by asking, "Can I tell you about my evening last night?" She proceeded to tell me how the Lord had set her completely free from her attachment to our house. It was really all right to sell. She didn't understand why she suddenly felt that way, but there seemed to be a breakthrough around 9:00 P.M.

Well, I could hardly see the road for tears, because it was at 9:00 P.M. that I had been praying for Bonnie. We serve an awesome God who is faithful to answer prayer. Don't waste your sorrows. God wants to use them.

At the meeting mentioned by Jack Munday, I described my dramatic reentry into the Numbered with the Transgressors principle, which I shared at the beginning of this book. I am not trying to use my experience to establish precedence, as though to bind it on others. However, the principle of identifying with others in prayer has proved valid in the experience of others such as Brother Munday. Many others have thanked me for clarifying their own experiences that were similar in nature. In some cases, their first response after hearing the Numbered with the Transgressors principle was to do nothing—which was their attempt to forget what happened. When the experience repeated itself, however, as it did with me, they began searching for answers.

The two scriptural references I have emphasized—Isaiah 53 and Romans 8—came to mind, once I turned my heart to God in search of some answers. We have discussed the text from Isaiah. Now it is time to understand why God gave me the other passage, Romans 8, which refers to the "groaning" Brother Munday heard at that meeting in Charlotte.

GROANING FOR OTHERS BY THE SPIRIT

In Romans 8:22-26, the apostle Paul tells the church of Rome that the entire creation groans in travail like the pangs of childbirth. He then goes on to explain that not only does all of creation travail, but the Church does also as we eagerly wait for God to complete His work on earth and take us home to be with Him.

> We know that the whole creation has been groaning as in the pains of childbirth right up to the present time. Not only so, but we ourselves, who have the firstfruits of the Spirit, groan inwardly as we wait eagerly for our adoption as sons, the redemption of our bodies. For in this hope we were saved. But hope that is seen is no hope at all. Who hopes for what he already has? But if we hope for what we do not yet have, we wait for it patiently. In the same way, the Spirit helps us in our weakness. We do not know what we ought to pray for, but the Spirit himself intercedes for us with groans that words cannot express.

Jesus taught us in the Gospels that the end would not come until all had heard the gospel: "And this gospel of the kingdom will be preached in the whole world as a testimony to all nations, and then the end will come" (Matt. 24:14). This proclamation of the gospel to all the world is one of the things for which we are to yearn.

Although the text from Paul was written to the church in Rome, I cannot find any evidence that the Church of our day is in this kind of travail. Since Paul's time, many major prayer ministries have mobilized worldwide prayer efforts. Yet a great portion of the Body of Christ is still standing outside this prayer movement.

The Holy Spirit is also a major part of this travailing intercession. The Spirit is the One who is praying through us in ways we never could. We are told in Romans 8:26 that the Holy Spirit helps us in our weakness (*KJV*, "infirmities"), making intercession for us with groanings that cannot be uttered. He does all this because we do not know what to pray for as we ought.

STRENGTH FOR OUR WEAKNESS

Now that we understand intercession, standing for those who cannot stand for themselves, we can focus our attention on the other parts of this passage. Notice the "weakness," which consists of infirmities that render us powerless to help ourselves. The Spirit helps our weaknesses and lack of power as He takes over the prayer time.

In Romans 15:1, we are told that the strong should bear the failings or infirmities of the weak. Not only does the Spirit help us, but we should also help others. How can we help anyone if we have infirmities ourselves, though? What we must investigate is how, or in what way, we are weak. The next sentence in Romans 8:26, in the *King James Version*, tells us that we are weak in that we do not know what to pray for *as we ought.*

We have some idea of what to pray for, because the areas of need are always before us. Problems abound in the communities in which we live. Family members are in need of prayer. Crime is everywhere and, to all appearances, there are no solutions. Abortion, drugs, a vacuum of leadership, gangs, problems in government, white-collar crime, organized crime, teen suicide, murders, rapes—the list goes on and on.

Our weakness is not being able to pray "as we ought"—which I believe implies that we are unable to pray from a place of feeling or identification with the people caught up in such problems.

The Bible says Christ was moved many times with compassion for those for whom He prayed. This compassion, which is not sympathy, but *anger* directed toward the true source of the problem, caused Him to bring a positive change to negative situations.

When we have personal problems in an area, we can feel the pain or the anxiety of not having an answer. When the problem belongs to someone else, however, at times we forget to pray after being asked. However, because of the Spirit's work, those things that concern us are ever before the face of God while we expectantly await the answer.

The Holy Spirit has the unique job of helping our weaknesses by allowing us to sense what a person is going through, thereby enabling us to pray with greater intensity. Much like the woman having a child, feelings play a large part in this process. She knows it is time to push when she feels the labor pains. If she is unable to feel the pains, someone has to tell her when to push.

Feelings are important if we are to identify with the problems of the people or situations around us. Remember, the man in the parable in Luke 11 had to help the powerless man get bread. The difference is we cannot rely on our human feelings during these times. We must allow the Holy Spirit to help us understand how the person feels or how the problem affects those around us. He is our helper in everything!

GROANING IN THE SPIRIT

The Spirit prays in groanings that cannot be expressed by humans alone. This is a deep cry, which means a great deal to God but could sound strange to people. When a woman is giving birth, the pains are very intense and observers may not fully identify with the woman's cries and groans. The greater the pain, though, the closer the child is to coming.

It is the same way in prayer. When the Spirit of God causes the groaning to start, the thing being prayed for is at hand. I have found this to be true during the seasons of prayer I have experienced. For example, in my experiencing the pain of homosexuality (chapter 1), it became clear to me that Father God had helped me in my inability (weakness or infirmity) to sense the need of homosexuals by allowing me to feel their pain and confusion and guilt.

Our entire lives are given over to the hands of the Holy

Spirit. He knows exactly what to pray to move the hand of God. He causes us to pray the Father's heart. This actually means the prayer focus was never really our idea. The Father needed someone to stand in the gap for something He wanted to change. Without our being touched with the infirmities, the prayer focus may not be accomplished.

Since this most important time in my life, 5 to 10 men have come to me seeking answers to the problem of homosexuality. I am grateful to God that I had already knocked on the door and had received bread. When my brother called me some two weeks after my prayer time for him, I had bread. The Father wanted someone to stand in the gap in these situations, and I was the one chosen.

DARING TO EXPECT RESULTS

Results always follow a time of intense intercession. As I speak on this principle in churches and conferences, the Body of Christ puts itself in the number when individuals pray for members of their natural family. They pray for an unsaved loved one. This time of prayer primarily focuses on prayers of mercy. The Holy Spirit then causes compassion to overtake the hearts of those praying and the intensity level immediately increases. I have included in this book several of the amazing results from these times of prayer.

God's heart is for the lost, and for everyone to come to the knowledge of His kingdom and His Christ. Will you dare to place yourself in the number, never to jump out again? If you will, you will see results, and the joy you experience will be full!

NOTES

Ministers — Stress

NOTES

NOTES

NOTES

NOTES

NOTES